Managing Your
First Years in Industry

Managing Your
First Years in Industry

*The Essential Guide to Career Transition
and Success*

David J. Wells

Clarkson University

IEEE
PRESS

The Institute of Electrical and Electronics Engineers, Inc., New York

This book may be purchased at a discount from the publisher when ordered in bulk quantities. For more information contact:

IEEE PRESS Marketing
Attn: Special Sales
P.O. Box 1331
445 Hoes Lane
Piscataway, NJ 08855-1331
Fax: (908) 981-8062

Printed in the United States of America
10 9 8 7 6 5 4 3 2 1

ISBN 0-7803-1021-7

IEEE Order Number: PP3707

Library of Congress Cataloging-in-Publication Data

Wells, David J.
    Managing your first years in industry : the essential guide to career transition and success / David J. Wells.
        p. cm.
    "IEEE United States Activities Board, sponsor."
    Includes bibliographical references and index.
    ISBN 0-7803-1021-7
    1. Engineers—Vocational guidance. 2. Career development.
    I. Institute of Electrical and Electronics Engineers. United States Activities Board. II. Title.
    TA157.W415 1995
    650.14'02462—dc20   94-29513
                                                                          CIP

for Bernd Selig and Fred Stern

This book could have been dedicated to Jane, but she deserves something far more personal than a dedication in a book on career management. *Managing Your First Years in Industry* is dedicated to two former bosses. Bernie Selig and Fred Stern are two of the most competent and capable individuals I have worked with. Their ability to manage in an environment of developing technology and troubled markets did not interfere with their abilities for leadership of people. They were each able to see to the individual betterment of those in their organizations in a manner that balanced the needs of the person with the demands of enterprise well. I considered them extremely tough and hard-driving at the time, yet they each maintained a high measure of loyalty and respect among the people they worked with and throughout the nuclear power services industry. The business saw remarkable strides as a result. It is their examples of leadership, when I worked in their respective organizations at CE Power Systems Group, to which I often turn for example and understanding.

Contents

Preface

This book on career management results from three influences of personal importance: my current responsibilities at Clarkson University as an academic program director and engineering educator, an extensive ongoing interface with industry through consulting, and the ever vivid recollection of my own career victories and dilemmas while in industry.

The differences between the worlds of education and industry are profound indeed; this is the heart of the challenge faced by graduates entering industry. My continuing interface among the constituencies of students, alumni, recruiters, and corporate executives forces a sort of triangulation on the issue of career management. Fortunately, each group values successful career starts. This interface, not without its pleasures, benefits effectiveness and serves to keep me honest.

Close parallels arise between the respective experiences of recent graduates and my own experiences several years earlier. The feelings of urgency, frustration, and exhilaration are all common companions to the evolution from student to leader. These feelings are strong motivators demanding attention. For me they encouraged an eventual respect, even a fondness, for competitive industry and free market competition. It seems that if career delays are to be avoided, it will be the result of greater understanding of the process of transition. *Managing Your First Years in Industry* seeks to address this need.

Effecting a successful transition seems quite simple, almost Darwinian in nature, yet career problems remain common, and effective help often seems remote. Few resources exist to help the individual understand the changes that must occur within. With two sides to the need for career success, it is natural for both the individual and upper management to hold a vested interest in developing a new hire's ability to contribute. This is a book on cooperation and mutual support between the manager and the new hire; it is written for them. To this end, it is intended that human resource and college placement personnel will also find this book a useful resource.

In education, the organization exists for the development of the individual. In industry, the individual exists for the well-being of the organization. From the individual's perspective, how can two worlds be much further apart? The complete shift in environment, motivation, reward, accountability, flexibility, and responsibility experienced by the recent graduate represents a fundamental paradigm shift that is not readily understood. Yet understanding is a prerequisite for progress. Therefore, it is no surprise, hopefully, that even the flow of money between person and organization reverses upon graduation—an indication of the magnitude of change occurring.

The résumé is one tool used in this book as a mechanism for helping the graduate consider new perspectives—those of management. Partly to scrutinize how a manager might evaluate an applicant, the greater objectives are helping the reader understand the needs of management and how to better relate one's qualifications to those real needs. The reader is invited to consider a functional view of himself or herself regarding accomplishments, abilities, and career interests. This serves to facilitate the needed paradigm shift. Given the success rates for graduates seeking to start their careers, the process seems to work well.

To help identify and avoid some of the more common predicaments encountered by college seniors and recent hires, case studies are used to illustrate the dynamics of career transition. A study of recent graduates of Clarkson University's Engineering and Management Program offers important perspective on career progress. Included are views on setting goals and achieving goals, factors that can help or hurt career progress when joining a new firm, valued traits of good companies and good management, career progress, and plans for graduate study. This study, conducted by Jody Dudley and myself, is summarized in Appendix A.

Of farther reaching interest, what can be done to accelerate the development of recent recruits into needed and valued contributors of design, management, and strategy? A program is suggested to involve the entire organization in the development of talent. The uniqueness of this program is that it forces the organization to close the feedback loop on employee development, and thus it imposes greater responsibilities on supervision for supporting development and on upper management for confirming that developmental goals are being met with each individual.

Managing Your First Years in Industry seeks to accomplish four goals. First is to help the reader more effectively articulate and, indeed, embrace his or her career goals and objectives. Next, it is beneficial for the graduate to adopt a functional view of their accomplishments, abilities, interests, and contributions. This aids their ability to relate well to the organization. The third goal to expedite the paradigm shift that must happen for the new hire to more readily assume the responsibilities they desire. The final goal is to help organizations succeed by more effectively developing the talent they dearly need.

Accordingly, it is a primary purpose of this book to help people, both individually and collectively, succeed through mutual support, cooperation, improved business awareness, and increased performance expectations.

The importance of feedback has been mentioned. You, the reader, can do much to further the development of this book as a resource for early career management by sharing your perspectives, experiences, and recommendations. Your input will be given careful consideration as subsequent editions are considered.

Dudley Kay, of IEEE Press, must be acknowledged for his encouragement to consider writing this book. Throughout the course of this effort he has continued to provide excellent advice and support, and I am grateful for his wonderful blend of encouragement and tolerance. Jack Housley and Bob Moran deserve thanks for their considerable assistance on a previous project which, in retrospect, provided much necessary groundwork for *Managing Your First Years in Industry*. Marion Beachley, Dave Schempp, Lee Svete, Ed Tierney, and Graham Wood took considerable time to review the manuscript, offer comment, and share ideas. Each an established leader, their assistance has been of considerable importance to this effort. I am also indebted to Catherine Avadikian, Bill Crittendon, Dave DiMaggio, Dave Holloway, Katheryn Johnson, Wayne Petzke, Rob Stavely, Scott Waring, Randy Waybright, and Scott Yager for their insights and support.

Jody Dudley's work, summarized in Appendix A, has been an important addition to the book. Chris McCamic's ability to prepare sketches and cartoons is greatly appreciated. Debbie McQuinn and Steve Hopkins both volunteered significant time and effort in providing a necessary critique of the manuscript draft. Lisa Mizrahi, Val Zaborski, and Kathy Coughlin effectively and efficiently helped me through review and production with well considered and constructive recommendations.

The many students, alumni, and recruiters who have been active participants in ongoing efforts and dialogue regarding career goals, job markets, and acclimation to the corporate environment have confirmed the importance of this effort and provided any sense of relevance contained in the following pages. There are others and I apologize for failing to mention them by name.

Foremost, I am grateful to Jane and our children, Jacob, Abbe, and Anastasia. At once they offer impelling incentives to work and to not work.

Dave Wells
Clarkson University

Chapter 1

Introduction

The difference between intelligence
and education is this: Intelligence will
make you a good living.

Charles F. Kettering

If not all careers seem important to you, certainly your own career is a most serious topic. You depend on it to provide a living and hope that it will offer satisfaction and growth opportunities as well. In fact, if you are an engineering student, your pursuit of higher education is exactly an effort to realize career opportunities in areas that hold personal interest—to do work that you enjoy.

Conversely, if you are a manager, you must locate, develop, and utilize technical talent to meet successfully the needs of your business. You are completely dependent upon the individuals in your organization. It is tough to find good talent, and it is time consuming and difficult to bring new hires fully on line within your business organization in a timely manner. Once you have developed the desired capabilities within your organization, you still have the continuing challenge of seeing that they are effectively used—this is why you are the manager. Recruiting failures, high attrition, and poor attitudes within your department are both expensive and troublesome; it is your responsibility to minimize their occurrence.

Regardless of whether you are a captain of industry or are

just getting started, you want your career to be successful, fulfilling, and enjoyable. The manager's success is drawn from the
talent in her organization, and the graduate's success follows his
or her ability to become a person within the organization considered to have talent. Whatever your responsibility, you both depend on the same thing—the successful development of new employees.

The early years of a career are fraught with obstacles and
uncertainty. When such concerns arise, they are sometimes expensive and generally uncomfortable, yet they are likely to be
your defining experiences as well. Although career problems in
the early years are manageable and frequently provide important experience, they are also often avoidable. Avoiding such difficulties allows you to apply your efforts toward the pursuit of
proactive efforts rather than reactive ones.

Communication failures are the predominant root of career
problems, particularly for starting engineers. Miscommunica-
tion compounds problems and obstructs your ability to recognize
problems and effect satisfactory remedies. An inability to effectively communicate with others will reduce your access to knowledge, responsibility, and opportunity at work. It is no surprise
that good communications skills are frequently identified as the
single most important attribute when extending an offer to a prospective employee.

DEFINITIONS OF CAREER SUCCESS: LET ME COUNT THE WAYS...

Management tends to overestimate the ability of new employees to navigate their careers safely and effectively within an organization. Whereas the manager takes the office rules and practices for granted, the new college graduate often has only classroom experiences as the primary model to follow. The roles and accountability of individuals in education differ completely from free-market industries. The shock of adapting to industry is often felt for several years by the graduate, even after promotion to initial supervisory responsibilities.

The career start following graduation often brings about changes such as relocation, marriage, starting a family, taking a mortgage, and even the purchase of a new automobile—all of which can have major impact on one's life. These events are all expensive and emotionally taxing, and they can focus the individual's attention unduly on salary growth. This result can distract the new engineer from paying sufficient attention to professional development, contribution at work, and seeking out the perspectives of others in the organization.

With very few exceptions, engineering careers commence within the framework of an organization in a subordinate role. For example, consulting, entrepreneurship, and strategic planning are not common entry-level endeavors. Instead, initial engineering positions are driven by the demands of the organization for work and require some minimum set of required skills. To fill these positions satisfactorily, the company must offer opportunities such as compensation, growth potential, and responsibility in order to attract the appropriate talent. The right talent has been documented in the form of education and experience and projects a compatible attitude. Obviously, the new employee has a complementary set of needs (money, et al.) and offerings (degree, et al.).

Once the employment contract is consummated, it is likely that the individual's needs and offerings will both grow! The result will be an effort to improve skills, gain experience, become more effective, and gain greater recognition within the organization.

Earning a college degree is a big step, but it is completed before the professional career starts. Experience in the analysis, design, and testing of a product is important and is garnered in industry. As a developing member of industry, the new engineer may wish to become established as a good writer, an effective contact for customer/clients, a project leader, and/or a capable business strategist. These additional capabilities increase the value of the individual to business.

What is in this for you? Growth in salary, responsibility, flexibility, and recognition are common. Let's face it, with an increased contribution at work, your job may become more interesting.

To some, this effort is a sacrifice of time and effort for a paycheck—a sordid view of life and work. Others see it differently—a natural system that encourages the individual to set and pursue career goals. Is it possible for companies and their employees both to be happy with their relationship by achieving individual goals as well as corporate goals? Yes! These may be the cornerstones of career success.

If the attainment of career success requires only that mutual care be taken by both the employee and the organization, what is the problem? For one thing, organizations are neither caring, intelligent, nor feeling. Consider the state and federal governments with their repertoire of programs and services to help citizens: Will a morning (mourning?) with the IRS and an afternoon with the department of motor vehicles convince you that they are working for your best interests? It is only through good leadership that an organization can effectively see to the needs of individuals (customers as well as employees), and the

care taken must emanate from an individual. Organizations that act or appear caring do so because it is the reflection of the will of leadership—individuals who care and who also have influence upon the organization.

New employees pose a challenge of their own to their employers. Just as a newborn baby cannot ask nicely for food or express gratitude when fed, new hires naturally care about their career development but often are unable to pursue effective courses of action and fail to mobilize the assistance of others, particularly that of their management. College graduates do not possess an a priori understanding of the organizational decision processes and human motivational skills that will allow them to excel in their responsibilities. These develop only with experience.

This book is aimed at those on both sides of the career challenge: The new employees and their management. Leaders and followers both must be productive in their roles, but they both depend upon the contributions of their counterparts to meet their objectives. A business filled with effective leaders and no followers is as useless as a business without leadership. Organizational effectiveness dictates the need for real-time feedback for both entities. The new employee holds obvious interest in making a successful go of his or her career, and management has the inescapable role of nurturing successful careers and employee development—after all, they pay a fortune for new employees.

First-level supervision would seem to be the facilitator of career success, but it seldom is. It is my observation that the primary task of supervisors is to see that work is satisfactorily completed to the last detail. They are also given the role of bringing new hires up to speed, but they encounter problems in fulfilling this role:

- Supervisors usually lack the requisite authority, preparation, sensitivity, and resources to successfully integrate their subordinates into the business.
- They are seldom held accountable for satisfactory employee development.
- It is difficult for supervisors to gain more than a narrow exposure to business issues. Thus, their understanding of business strategy is necessarily limited and likely flawed.

For the supervisor who is still reading, you have neither the excuse of being a new employee nor the authority of an established leader; you are assigned to the bureaucratic purgatory of free enterprise. Do not let management relegate you to a narrow business function and give you limited resources for personnel development. The only way out is for you to become better than the typical demands of your position!

The term management, as used throughout the book, refers to all levels of management actively engaged in business strategy and leadership of people. Because I do not hold the hope that supervision can reliably assume the responsibilities of upper management in developing talent, supervision is not considered to be among the ranks of management. The higher levels of management hold the vision, the funds, the strategic involvement, and the recognized need for developing good talent well. They may become too occupied with other matters to address the needs of their new hires, but the accountability and responsibility are theirs alone.

José Rivera graduated from the university last year with a degree in electrical engineering and accepted a position with the company of his first choice. He has an outstanding work ethic and has exceeded his supervisor's expectations for quality, quantity, and timeliness of work. José also gets along well with his peers.

When José was hired, he was led to expect a review and a raise in six months. A promotion and another raise could happen as early as his first anniversary if he met performance expectations and established himself as part of the team. Cheryl Crow is his supervisor and has more than twenty years of experience. Cheryl is not responsible for making salary and promotion decisions. These decisions are made by Ms. Susan Van Vleet, the departmental manager, with the approval of Mr. Aaron Bloom, the vice president. José has not received any significant feedback from his supervisor regarding job performance. In fact, the mandatory performance review meeting, referred to as a formality by Cheryl, still has not been scheduled.

One major contract is almost complete, and the current backlog of work for the department is lower than it has been. Even though a number of proposals for additional work are under active consideration, no new contracts have been awarded for quite some time. The division is waiting to make a decision on all but the essential raises and promotions. No announcements have been made regarding reviews, raises, and promotions. Aaron,

Susan, and Cheryl have all been through this kind of business cycle several times before, and they know enough to wait it out.

José is still the "new hire," and this is the first time in his life that his work has not been rewarded on schedule. In addition, he sees that his living expenses are eating up most of his paycheck, and he does not have the discretionary funds he was looking forward to. A raise is becoming more important to him, and he is starting to believe that the company is taking advantage of him. Perhaps his future with this company is not as bright as it once looked. Cheryl sometimes hears an edge in José's comments, but José will just have to grow up. Susan remembers interviewing José but has not had the time to talk with him since José's first week at work. She has heard that José is working well and is aware of no problems. Right now, Susan's focus is on next year's labor forecast, and she does not have all of the information she needs to complete his submittal.

> *The older I grow, the more I listen to people who don't say much.*
> Germaine G. Glidden

There are clouds on the horizon of José's career. It is a common scenario, and several observations are worth noting:

- José does not sense his value within the organization.
- José has failed to express his growing concerns to his supervision and management.
- Cheryl and Susan are also not communicating well with José.
- José now sees his role at work as somewhat adversarial; one gains at the expense of the other.

Consider the issues from an organizational perspective. A company is a collection of individual and business interests that are compatible, active, and self-supporting. Individual or personal interests are held by employees, owners, customers, and perhaps others, such as suppliers and community neighbors. The primary interests of organizations include return on investment, growth, reputation, technology, and market performance, to mention a few. A firm's product (i.e., automobiles, airplanes, computers, pumps, advice) is exchanged for the money used to meet the financial needs of the organization and its people.

As such, it must be remembered that engineering is a subset of business activity. An organization may include engineers who contribute to the design, manufacture, and service of a product, but seldom are engineering and/or engineers the sole product of an industrial firm. Thus, one must think of the discipline within the context of service to industry. Also, it is not likely that an engineer will become independently employed (i.e., as a consultant or self-employed) until significant experience is garnered in the setting of an industrial organization.

A couple of points might be made regarding enterprise:

Organizations ought to have a mission, goals, and a plan. They are the prerequisite for understanding growth possibilities and measuring performance. In effect, they are the company's rudder. Without it, all progress is luck. In addition to providing a benchmark for accountability, strategic plans, goals, and a mission serve to align the diversely populated groups of an organization toward common purposes.

In order to thrive, the firm must understand markets and competition. Markets define the need for products, technology, and service. Companies learn what new offerings to consider and what their potential value in the marketplace is. Once a new market opportunity is identified, free-market trade will determine the profit potential of that market based upon the demand and competitive factors such as product quality, availability, pricing, and manufacturing cost.

It is not sufficient that only a few leaders within a company understand markets and competition. This knowledge ought to be shared, discussed, and understood among employees at all levels.

The company must remain financially viable. Good plans, good markets, and good people are not enough to float an organization when the money runs out. Financial cushions are helpful for four reasons:

1. To increase stockholder equity: Stockholders fund an organization with the hope of gaining a return on their investment. The value of their continued financial support must remain evident.

2. To weather financial storms: Markets, economies, and costs can change significantly in ways that can reduce cash flow. Problems can arise that draw upon financial reserves. Examples include fire and flood losses, departure of key personnel, and environmental, labor, or legal problems.

3. To pursue opportunity: The availability of money provides flexibility for the organization to pursue opportunities when they arise, whether it is facilities expansion, product development, or the acquisition of another business.

4. To save money and maintain control: Borrowed money is financially expensive and can increase the control of outsiders over your business.

Resources and processes should be improved. Increased efficiency, reduced scrap, improved safety, and more effective market penetration all contribute to increased revenues or decreased costs. Developmental programs can encourage improvements in equipment and process performance, but such programs can attain success only by effectively equipping and encouraging employees to identify and address such opportunities.

Employee motivation must be a priority. What can be done to help people meet their responsibilities and strive for growth? In order to meet their basic responsibilities, they can achieve no job satisfaction until they are at least minimally qualified to do their jobs. Beyond that, it is as necessary to develop the person as an individual as it is for the person to grow in the business. It is critical that this dual purpose be apparent to the employee. Management must understand what their employees seek out of their life's work. They should encourage employees to seek more rather than less out of their careers; finally, management ought to facilitate the employee's pursuit of growth.

If businesses should maintain their goals as understandable, compatible, and, preferably, complementary with personal goals, it is likewise meaningful for the employee or individual to align his or her personal goals with corporate needs. Understanding corporate goals and relating them to personal goals can improve employee attitudes. Of course, the role of communication remains evident here, because individuals have a tendency to misunderstand and mistrust corporate goals when an adequate understanding has not been achieved.

As José approaches his first anniversary, his situation seems to offer little hope. He has become increasingly dissatisfied and is now focused on changing employers. His employer has come to see José as having somewhat of an attitude problem and feels that the department may be as well off without him. In their minds, hiring José may have been a mistake—particularly at a time when the issues at hand are so pressing.

If they replace José, they will lose a total of two years—the six months it took to recruit José and get him on board, the year he spent on payroll before leaving, and the six months it will take to replace him. The financial load (a year of salary and benefits, moving expenses, training costs, and the customary recruiting expenses for filling a position twice) will also be considerable, particularly while business is slow. Even worse, if they lose José, they may not be allowed to fill the position until after new work is contracted.

José thinks that he also has made a mistake in taking this position. A year has passed, and he does not have much to show for it. It will be more difficult getting a job when having to explain such a short period of employment with his first employer. José is carrying a lot of anxiety and sees this experience as his first failure. Further, his job search effort is directed more toward getting away from his current employer, and he is not putting much rational thought into characterizing the position that offers him the brighter future he wants. At this point, José is running scared, and any new job opportunity looks like a good one.

This relationship has proceeded blindly to a seemingly unresolvable state. In summary:

- José is fully dissatisfied at work, sees no future with his current employer, and is looking for any way out.
- José lacks the necessary direction and maturity for managing a positive career change.

- Management is unhappy with José, yet they fail to assume their responsibility in José's successful development.

Is it likely that José will conduct a successful job search? Probably not. Also, his management probably recognizes his desire for a change and hopes that he resigns before they have to face the messy task of letting him go. Regardless, both will pay a price.

This is not an ideal start for a career, yet many good people face exactly these types of problems during their initial years after college. What is more, this situation could have been completely avoided with discussion among employee and management—a solution requiring no funding, only care. José had twelve months on the job with an apparently good initial start; why didn't José and management talk? José lacks the maturity and his management lacks the vision, competence, and care to see that José's career progress stays on track. Neither party adequately watched out for José, nor did they effectively tend to business needs.

The emotional expense is obvious. If problems such as this extend beyond one or two isolated individuals, their negative attitudes can permeate an entire department. The organizational need to develop good functional talent for the long run is impeded, and the financial performance desired by the owners is adversely impacted. When near-term goals and short-sightedness get in the way of long-range strategy, people and organizations both suffer.

Engineers have a well-deserved reputation for being able to grow in—and broaden—their careers, yet they also show a vulnerability for early problems. In fact, the characteristic factors that work to their favor in one sense pose difficulty as well.

1. The ability to focus on technical problems requires a disciplined approach that puts extraneous information aside. As a result, the tasks of preference, although possibly complex, are often "clean"; they avoid the uncertainties that make closed solutions unlikely—issues including the market, money, people, and motivation. In industry, structural changes have occurred that open new worlds to the engineer—increasing exposure and responsibility

beyond the traditional responsibilities of design, analysis, and testing. It is not that these traditional responsibilities are supplanted; rather, engineers must better relate the fruits of their labors to the business world about them.

2. A belief in the value of cold logic for approaching problems is conditioned over the entire course of an engineering education. It fosters a confidence and discipline to tackle tough problems but can extend to the sole reliance upon logic for selling ideas to management. "If you can't find a flaw in my logic, then you have to accept my ideas." This, of course, overlooks the need to have others find your ideas likeable as well as logical. For example, your stated reasons for buying a particular car are that it has a reputation for reliability, the dealer provides good service, and the price is excellent. Let's face it, you bought the car because it is red, goes fast, and looks great. Logic is often used to defend a decision that has already been made emotionally.

3. Engineers are conditioned to expect steady progress as long as they keep getting the right answers. This expectation is nurtured throughout their college education, and why shouldn't it be? Diligence always provides the solution to a problem. In course after course, year after year, the student realizes constant progress as long as the work is satisfactorily completed. Given a seventeen-year period of conditioning, how can the new graduate anticipate any difference in the realization of career growth? Until this perception is remedied, one might expect considerable job-related frustration.

4. "Tune out everything but the problem at hand." At one well-known company in New England, with a beautiful campus setting, are approximately 2500 engineers. It is an excellent place to work, and the breadth of talent is truly amazing. I worked there for awhile and have always been grateful for the opportunities afforded in working with outstanding individuals on fascinating problems while having access to excellent resources. At times, I

would have visitors on site and enjoyed showing them some of the interesting projects in progress as well as the lovely setting with walkways around the pond. On a nice day, we would see turtles, butterflies, snakes, birds, and catfish—a gorgeous pastoral setting for work. There would always be other individuals strolling on the paths, and, frequently, they would be looking down (at their feet? into space?) as they sauntered along. Sometimes the guests were in sales and could not resist greeting every single person they passed. If these people lacked exposure to engineers, they often expressed common observations, "What in hell is the matter with these guys? Everyone walks around looking at the ground, and nobody responds to my greetings."

Engineering, as a discipline, requires mental concentration to solve problems and great mental concentration for solving great problems. Of course, the bigger the problem, the better the resulting accomplishment. Thus, a number of us were in deep thought (or tried to be)—a funk, perhaps, if I am to believe my closest relatives. I recall similar situations in other organizations as well and believe that engineers, in particular, are prone to address other challenges in much the same fashion to the point of seeming distant or inattentive to those around them. As students, engineers are conditioned to look within for reason and are not often encouraged to understand or respect other issues of importance that may relate to others—employees, customers, or stockholders.

In engineering education, as well, I enjoyed the responsibilities and opportunities that were available. Regardless, I am continually amazed at the limits that many engineers seem to place on the value of their own discipline. Perhaps too many engineering programs impose only the expectation that graduates will become good engineers and fail to include the expectation that students will develop into good leaders as well. The world usually needs good engineers, but those who can also lead will be in much higher demand, will be much more influential, and will experience much greater career flexibility.

The successful engineering career requires much more than technical ability. One must develop a broad awareness for the

mission of the organization and an ability to develop and promote ideas that are compatible with the business strategy. Engineers, if they wish to lead, must learn to manage their own tasks
and promote their own ideas first. Failing this, they are relegated
to micromanagement by others, and they will be allowed to do
only what others tell them to. This is not to state that all engineers must learn how to manage others, but minimally they ought
to be able to manage their own work and project themselves as
capable engineers.

When engineers' career potentials are not realized, it may
be because they limit themselves too much to a technical perspective. Failing to respect the strategic business issues will preclude participation in strategic business decisions. It is on the
engineer's shoulders to go beyond the boundaries of a traditional
engineering education if his or her aspiration is for leadership,
strategy, and business competitiveness.

In order to bridge the communications gap, this book views
career growth from the perspectives of the organization and the
individual. Regardless of your current level of responsibility, both
perspectives are worth consideration.

The book *Working*, by Studs Terkel (1974), offers a broad,
but fascinating, view into the lives and perceptions of people who
work. Its major omission, in my opinion, is that few professionals are included, and there are relatively few examples of individuals who delight in their work. There may be a lot of unhappy
workers on the job, but one reason for pursuing an education is
to transcend some of the mundane chores and become involved
in a particular area that interests you. The book is well worth
reading, if only to gain new perspectives on how people are moti-
vated or demotivated.

A study of recent graduates of Clarkson University's Interdisciplinary Engineering and Management during the first five
years of their careers is quite encouraging. Respondents volunteered their views on career satisfaction, and 94 percent of the
respondents felt they were making progress toward their goals.
Figure 1.1 shows voluntary responses regarding career satisfaction (the voluntary responses of meeting career goals is in addition to the specific question asked of all respondents that identified 94 percent as making progress). (See Appendix A.)

I am contacted regularly by individuals seeking career ad-

Most satisfying aspects of work
Responses to open-ended questions

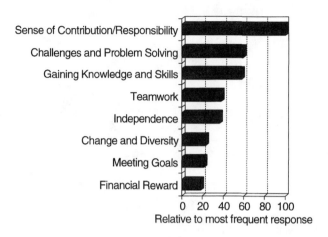

Figure 1.1 Career Satisfaction

vice. Most are in the first couple of years in their careers and do not understand how to overcome job-related problems effectively. These people always ask few questions regarding a particular situation at work before the real issue arises—finding another job. They are often convinced that no further opportunities exist with their current employers and a job change offers the only real growth opportunity. Actually, I like these calls. Once they personally experience a dilemma at work, people are much more willing to seek out other perspectives (particularly third-party perspectives).

Memories of my own experiences regarding similar problems remain vivid, and I believe that many capable individuals feel thwarted in the initial years of their career. For lack of experience, maturity, and perspective, such feelings are frequently of our own doing.

This book seeks to help employees and management avoid misunderstandings. When issues do arise, approaches are proposed that can be initiated by either party to effectively address problems. Whether the approach is avoidance or corrective action, success hinges upon a mutual respect and understanding among an organization's members—qualities that are engendered only through earnest communications.

Chapter 2

What Students Need to Know Beyond Their Education

The degree of one's emotion varies
inversely with one's knowledge of
the facts—the less you know the
hotter you get.

Bertrand Russell

The Searching Senior

High school students, when applying for college, may have hand-written their applications while sitting around in a T-shirt and jeans. Mom and Dad helped see that the bills got paid as long as academic performance was acceptable. As the transition to industry nears, things change. The job application includes a polished résumé, and much care goes into selecting a new suit of clothes for interviewing. It is a time to consider what is acceptable and attainable with regard to wages, responsibilities, location, and so on. Family and friends take an interest in how the senior will pursue a career. A new task is at hand, and the big test is finding a "good job." The whole world is watching.

Tim O'Hara is a senior engineering student who has performed reasonably well in his academic program. He has always been a strong student, and this is an important accomplishment in his mind because many of the other students in his class have had more hands-on experience than he prior to entering college. Tim's other pursuit, competitive gymnastics, is one where he has attained national ranking. While growing up, he just did not have the time to gain hands-on, or relevant, work experience. Nevertheless, Tim is near the top of his class and has developed a good sense for applied engineering through his involvement with society competitions.

After a successful seventeen years of education and twelve years of competitive sports, Tim is now facing one of those big life changes—completing his education and commencing his career in industry. Each year, he completed the necessary academic tasks satisfactorily and proceeded to the next level. In his mind, he sees graduation and the start of a new job as only an extension of his education. In school, he was grouped with a number of other individuals who also had the ambition to pursue engineering, and each of the forty or more courses that he has completed represents a success on his part. Many of the courses were not easy and some were not enjoyable, yet he persevered. In short, he attained a number of minor milestones as well as a few major ones. The B.S. degree will signal his establishment as an engineer. He has learned to work well with faculty and knows how to listen, to understand and follow directions, and to satisfy course requirements without excessive effort.

Tim expects to do well in his career search because of his academic performance. His athletic accomplishments should project him as being self-disciplined, yet well rounded. He has not set specific targets for job responsibilities and environment; Tim is keeping himself open for all possibilities. He does expect a good salary and assumes that his career direction will sort itself out. He understands that most companies claim career flexibility for new employees, and their training programs are designed to allow him to window shop while he gains some exposure to the work place. Eventually, he hopes to have his own business.

Interviewing seems to have proceeded well, with more than a dozen under his belt. He enjoys visiting with the recruiters and learning about different industries, but no job trips or likely prospects have arisen, only stall letters and rejections. He is upset with some of the companies because they have extended offers to classmates whose academic performance is not as strong. Tim is ready to make some big bucks, and he wants to accept a position so he can claim success at this point. He has decided to buy a new car to mark this event.

The recruiting season is about two-thirds over, and Tim has not found a job or a company that excites him. He wants to proceed with his plans of gaining some kind of experience but is at a loss in explaining the lack of success in his search. Everything seems to be blocking his plans to make a career decision and buy a car.

Tim's classmate, Martha Chandler, has interviewed with many of the same companies as Tim. Her academic performance is not quite as strong as his, but she has done reasonably well. Still, Martha was nervous about her grades. Martha likes construction and wants to be a project engineer. Over the period of two summers, she worked for a construction firm and loved it. Her interviews have gone well, and she is excited about the opportunities she sees on the outside. She cannot wait to get college behind her and go to work. This was apparent to the interviewers, and Martha now has two employment offers. Martha is ready to make her decision.

The role of communication skills, career objectives, and attitude is apparent. Tim has not found his reason for going to work, or is it that the recruiters have not found a reason to put him to work? Tim may indeed encounter his first major failure. He has learned the process for being successful in school but does not know how to communicate with others, particularly those in industry. Interviewers have enjoyed their visits with him, but they have been only visits. He shows no passion for his career, and although several recruiters have stated that he should give further thought to his career objectives, their recommendations have gone by him completely. For Tim, any career prospects in industry seem like a letdown from the successes he has enjoyed at college.

It would be wrong to assume that Martha received offers because of gender issues. Although many consider the construction industry to be male-dominant, Martha shows a direction and enthusiasm for her career that is infectious. Recruiters are attracted to this enthusiasm and have full confidence that Martha will be well received and will meet the demands of the job. Even though some other candidates show stronger academic performance, the recruiters have greater confidence in her potential for success.

Tim and Martha were both diligent in working with their placement office to prepare for their search. They were given an extensive amount of information and advice, and both Tim and Martha went through similar processes in conducting their search preparations.

The important differences between Martha and Tim are not academic performance or preparation. From the recruiters' perspectives, a fundamental difference in attitude and career direction is the key. Martha benefited from her work experience in setting her career direction. The combination of direction and attitude is immensely helpful, but it is far less common than might be expected. Accordingly, one person has offers, and the other does not.

A change of focus occurs in the senior year as students shift their attention from course work to careers. Even if the student is not exactly sure of his or her career plans and objectives, the senior year is monumental for engineering students because they are expected to be successful. I have held panel discussions for entering first-year students and made the mistake of filling the panel only with seniors. I thought discussion would focus on projects, study abroad, Greek organizations, and how to enjoy college.

It was as if the seniors were speaking a foreign language. A question was asked regarding the selection of elective courses. Almost immediately the panel response diverted to the topics of career goals and job search strategies. Over and over, in spite of the variety of questions posed by entering students and my own protests, the panel responses returned to the search! That panel was certainly mission-oriented, and their mission had little to do with the incoming students, whose mission was to acclimate to college and make the most of it. I do not imagine that the job search mentality was very interesting to the incoming students, and, needless to say, subsequent panels were not exclusively seniors.

The Intermediaries

To get to the point of having a job, the student will probably be involved with two intermediaries—the college's placement office and the prospective employer's human resources (or personnel) office. Essentially, the placement office works as an agent for the student, whereas HR represents the employer's interests.

College Placement and Career Development Offices

College placement and career development offices have the immense task of facilitating the successful transition of individuals from college to employment. They assist college juniors and seniors in their preparations and provide the facilities and support for on-campus interviewing. Letter writing, interviewing, résumés, dress, search strategies, and, naturally, career planning are typical areas for the placement office to address with the student. The role of motivator is central to helping students present themselves in the best possible light to potential employers. In fact, it is not unusual for the placement office to assume the larger burden of "explaining the real world" to the student. Placement offices also seek corporate recruiters for on-campus recruiting. The placement effort is considered successful when both the student and the recruiter are both pleased with their interview.

In the past several years placement personnel have more aggressively developed programs to help students with their decision processes and tactical planning for the search effort. Alumni and/or recruiters are utilized in panel discussions to address the changes awaiting college graduates, and some placement offices have extended their services to assist alumni with career/employment changes occurring after the experience of the first job. Successes in this area exist, but the abilities of a college or university to promote available alumni effectively and broadly within industry are limited. I should expect this area of activity will meet specific needs from time to time, but it is not likely to develop into a large and broadly effective effort at many universities.

Human Resources (HR)

Human resources personnel typically control the on-campus recruiting efforts of a prospective employer. From a business perspective, recruiting is a relatively small component of the HR function. Their other responsibilities are to administer personnel policy, promotions, salary increases, and benefits (insurance, vacation, and stock options) and to address employee problems. To the college senior, HR is often the first and predominant point of contact with prospective employers. Sometimes, HR is the only source of information regarding a particular position.

HR sees to it that the recruiting process remains consistent and, one hopes, effective. Operating units with open positions usually do not have the time or ability to recruit talent. HR saves them a lot of time and expense by automating the recruiting process on a larger scale than any single department can implement. Laws impacting employment and hiring have grown to the point where individual operating units can no longer effectively implement recruiting programs that are fully satisfactory.

HR runs interference for the operating units. With a consolidated recruiting effort, it is much more difficult for job applicants to meet with individuals from the operating units that may have suitable positions open for them. Those managers are often too busy managing; they are just as happy that HR conducts the initial screening of applicants.

A particularly dim view of HR's recruiting role, offered by Tom Daust (1990) is that HR is both weak and deadly. It is weak because it has no authority to extend an offer—that decision is made by the line organizations and operating groups who need talent. HR only screens applicants to determine who will receive further consideration. HR is deadly because it does screen applicants—HR can kill an application before it receives any consideration by someone who might hold both the ability and insight to extend an offer.

Students tend to misread job opportunities and misrepresent themselves because they are outside of their element in the industrial employment market. For this reason, they frequently encounter failure in their search efforts, particularly when the job market is slow. Industrial experience provides a framework for assessing the merits of various opportunities and exposure that students often lack. Second, students are communicating through intermediaries, each placing their own "spin" on the various position openings. It is a vulnerable process. Some difficulties are these:

The career search is viewed by students as another course to be passed. As such, they may pursue a mechanistic approach to their search and never give their own values and interests the consideration due. This does not engender conviction toward specific career paths. Instead, the search is seen as a grand chess game with a raft of intricate rules. Students tend to focus more on the rules and recommendations of the process than on earnest person-to-person communications with prospective employers. Students with quality work experience, such as a co-op work position can provide, are often able to overcome this difficulty.

Too much emphasis is placed on getting a job offer. The strategy and effort needed for locating a position are quite consuming and can distract the individual from considering what life will be like after an offer is received. As such, all efforts are directed at getting job offers, with little consideration being given to the particular opportunities and challenges associated with specific positions, departments, supervision, and the like. It is not unusual for new employees to be completely surprised by the work requirements, routine, and environment. A singular focus on "getting the offer" is largely to blame.

The intermediaries want you to like them. HR and your placement office both want you to like the employment opportunities you have access to. Even though the interviewers may not give your application further consideration, they will always want you to have high regard for their companies. As recruiters, it is their responsibility to be an advocate for their employers. The placement office tends to be more balanced; they are advocates for students and employers alike. The placement office is unlikely to recommend in favor of specific offers and employers, nor should they recommend particular students, but they naturally want visiting companies and students to like each other. The recruiting com-

panies and the placement office both actively seek to promote their good names.

The intermediaries want you to say yes. The time comes
when companies start to extend offers for employment. At
this point, the recruiter and the placement office want you
to accept the offer. After all, when you agree to an employment offer, you have made the placement office and the recruiter successful in their mission! The placement office may
not tell you to accept the offer, but it does want its students
placed by the end of the year, and it does not want good positions going to students at other universities. This adds to
the already increasing pressure for you to say yes.

*The intermediaries often promote a distorted view of indus-
try.* HR is ancillary to the primary business operations of
the firm. For this reason, it probably does not have an adequate basis for understanding the day-to-day business practices and decisions. After all, it does not design, it does not
manufacture, it is not involved with market strategy, and it
does not work with the customers. HR is telling you only
what it hears from the firm's operating groups. Also, because it wishes to present the firm in the best light and wants
you to favor any employment opportunities that may arise,
it is apt to be telling you what you want to hear.

The college placement office is also naturally limited in its
functional awareness of how recruiting companies operate and
make decisions. Human Resources and your college placement
office both provide you with important information and access to
employment opportunities. You need to recognize how these intermediaries alter your perception of job possibilities open to you.
You also need to talk to people who directly oversee the functional responsibilities you are seeking.

The placement office at the university where I work has
maintained an excellent reputation. It does well in drawing good
companies to campus for recruiting, and it provides extensive
support in helping students pursue job opportunities in their
fields. Yet it is interesting to note occasions where the placement
office may be a victim of it's own success. In the college environment, seniors frequently fail to recognize that the responsibility
for finding a good job is not with the placement office, and it is

not up to Mom and Dad. They are aware of the success of the placement office and fully expect that the transition to industry will follow naturally and successfully. It seems that many must first encounter clear personal failure in their search efforts before they are willing to draw upon the resources at hand.

As we see with Tim, there are seniors who perceive that their most significant accomplishment is largely behind them. Career opportunities may not seem to hold the charm that college life has. Let us face it, we had a lot of fun in college! Making a successful transition into a career is the very next goal, yet it can become the very first personal failure. If so, it will not be a small one; it is the kind of catastrophe that can overshadow all prior successes.

It is at the end of the senior year that many students find out that a set of rules (in the form of advice) is just not enough to get a good job. By then, seniors are facing the crunch—final exams and commencement—and then they go home! Monday morning after commencement will arrive, and the new graduate will sit across the breakfast table from Mom or Dad. The graduate will not have a clue as to what to do next to find a good job, and Mom and Dad may not either. Dad and Mom will have read the résumé with pride and wonder at the injustice of the graduate's unemployment.

The stress resulting from these circumstances precipitates profound change for the graduate. For the first time, he or she recognizes that the rules have changed, and he or she is losing. It is time for fundamental questions and honest answers.

Why Work?

For reasons that can only be surmised, career endeavors often do not look as enjoyable or stimulating as college life. The obvious career measurables in industry are salary and position. To the student, they may seem analogous to grade-point average and class year. One might then define employment as the surrender of time and effort for pay. If the work is not so fulfilling, students and recent graduates may hold the notion that sufficient spending money can more than offset this concern. It is to be hoped that this destructive view of work will be corrected at some point in the graduates' careers. For the time being, a desire or need for money is often the initial motivator forcing seniors to commence their search. The need for money may motivate a person to look for work, but it offers no reason for the employer to extend an offer. It is a reason why college students and recent graduates so often fly blind in their career search.

This leads to the question, Why leave college to work? Without a graduate's having a heartfelt reason for commencing a career, what reason can a company have for extending an offer? These seniors have no clear objectives and have identified no aspects of a career that look exciting, except pay. They cling to the hope that they can bluff their way into a job. It is at this point that a more accurate and more workable definition of career success must be established.

To help students to recognize possible weaknesses in their career search efforts, I ask a class to list the characteristics of a good job. Although students express a number of characteristics, the first and easiest answer invariably is a high starting salary. After presenting this question and hearing the response, I give an example for consideration.

In this example, I am staffing an organization that produces and markets breakfast cereal. The student who first identified salary as being the most important characteristic of an opportunity is selected to fill the first, and highest-paying, position in the firm. That person will have a brand-new office and a personal secretary and will receive a starting annual salary of $70,000. The responsibilities are quite simple; the individual's likeness will be used on the box of cereal for promotional purposes. To sweeten the deal even further, the recruit understands that he or she will receive a 15 percent salary increase within six months if sales increase at all. Projected sales look very promising, so an increase seems likely.

In this model, other students are hired as well, but their responsibilities and salary differ from those of the first person hired. They are given responsibilities in roles including product research, process design, production, marketing, finance, and quality, to mention a few. These new employees have starting salaries between $25,000 and $35,000.

There is a condition. The high-paid (and, it is hoped, photogenic) recruit must keep to his or her well-furnished office and stay out of the way of those who have real work to do. Even though the other employees are each earning less than half of the star's salary, it is their responsibility to run the business, produce the product, maintain quality, improve efficiency, meet sales and margin goals, and make all the day-to-day operational decisions.

Although most seniors indicate a desire for a high salary, this single condition makes this unique opportunity fully unacceptable for them. After all, this offer carries an embedded challenge to one's ability to make a meaningful contribution at work through thought and labor. Further, there is almost immediate resentment among the other employees regarding the one "standout." This resentment also is unacceptable to the individual who has been employed only for image reasons.

The point of the preceding scenario is that many college seniors have a gross misunderstanding of what employers need. Under these circumstances, students are fully ineffectual in offering prospective employers any value.

One option for deferring the question of work is graduate school. Some know exactly what they want out of their graduate education and make good choices in following that path. Many others consider further studies after graduation only as a way to stay in a known environment and either defer the real decisions regarding one's career or cope with a lack of success in the search.

What About Graduate School?

The pursuit of a graduate education is a highly individualized issue. An increasing number of college graduates pursue additional education, but each must determine his or her own reasons. Probably the most common and least justified reason is that the additional degree will help the graduate get a good job—absolutely the wrong reason for pursuing graduate studies!

It is frequently recommended that graduate studies be pursued after some career experience has been gained. Many have found that career responsibilities did the most to help them clarify their career objectives and plans. Given that the proportion of individuals who have clear objectives more than doubles during the first five years following college, it is no surprise that this period defines their needs for additional education as well. It is a period where individuals may develop career objectives in areas as diverse as technology, finance, law, management, or marketing. An exception occurs when a student has a good co-op work experience that has helped the individual set clear and deliberate graduate school plans.

In the Dudley-Wells study, ninety percent of a group of recent graduates considered graduate studies important (Figure 2.1). However, the recommendation to gain experience first as a mechanism for selecting the appropriate path of graduate studies was advocated by a margin of eight to one. When asked to explain their views on pursuing graduate studies directly after completing undergraduate work, the following comments were offered:

- *It takes "getting your feet wet" before you can get a grasp on what opportunities exist and how to pursue them.*

- *Graduate studies are important if they allow the individual to obtain a job that is important to him or her and would not be possible otherwise. If an individual is not 100 percent certain where he or she wants to be, experience is a better choice than graduate work.*

- *Several years of work experience should allow the individual to better relate the content of a graduate education to the demands of industry.*

- *Although it is helpful to have a base of experience before going to grad school, it is very difficult to give up the financial security of a permanent position. I recommend getting two to three years of professional experience to define future goals more clearly.*

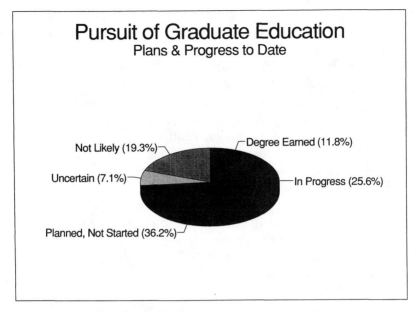

Figure 2.1   Pie chart on graduate study

The question "Why leave college?" remains relevant. If students are not sold on the concept of going to work for more than a mere salary, it is highly unlikely that they will be successful in convincing any recruiter to offer them an opportunity. It is at this point that the student must develop a more accurate, a more focused, and a more workable definition of career success.

What Is Career Success?

Most college students want career success; they simply cannot articulate what success means. A large part of the search in the beginning is to establish a personally acceptable definition of career success. Until a workable definition of success is found, all career goals are ill defined and difficult to attain. Under these circumstances, success happens only through luck. Luck is good to hope for but terrible to rely upon. Of course, once you have a clear definition of career success, your motivation to attain it increases. It is also likely that your personal definition of career success will be continually modified as you attain goals and gain experience. Experience will temper such definitions throughout your career, and perhaps they will converge on some central definition.

Although salary and position may be the most readily expressed components of career success, the Dudley-Wells study indicates they are not sufficient in themselves to provide job satisfaction (Appendix A). They do not offer the incentive and enjoyment for the hard work that is required to attain such a definition. This success definition of fame and fortune, in addition to being misleading, is largely unattainable as a primary goal!

Finding a better definition is not so difficult—ask a large group of individuals if they consider themselves successful in their careers. For those that do, ask them to define success. The results fit well with common sense. Recent graduates demonstrate a marked shift in their definitions of career success.

Enjoyment

Not all jobs are fun, nor are there any that are fun all of the time, but you have the right to expect enjoyment from your career. The job is right when you look forward to going to work, when you respect the people you work with, and when you have a shared sense of personal, as well as organizational, mission. Of course, these kinds of jobs are not handed to you; they must be developed. If your current position fails to meet these minimum standards, you may wish to consider what steps you can take to improve your work environment before deciding that a job change is the only solution.

Sense of Contribution

Is a sense of contribution more important than enjoyment, or is this merely a contributor to enjoyment? Certainly, when a sense of contribution is not present, job satisfaction is unlikely. It is remarkable to observe a recent hire when he or she is congratulated for an important job well done. It is as strong a motivator as I have seen, and it may explain why, in part, so many of my generation became what they said they would not be—committed to their careers! When the organization values the result of your hard work, then your time and labor are validated. It becomes at least one reason for existence. As your abilities develop to make further contributions, you establish yourself as being uniquely qualified—perhaps even irreplaceable in the eyes of management. It is not a bad position to be in.

Flexibility

Companies change, management changes, and people change. You too are likely to change throughout your career. These changes will encompass interests, abilities, and goals. From a student's view, careers often look so static, yet nothing could be further from the truth. You will want as much career flexibility as you can get. This flexibility allows you to assume other responsibilities in an organization; it can allow you to change jobs, companies, and industries. As your interests develop and change, the job that was once so attractive will lose its fascination. Both you and your company will be better off if you strive to develop your abilities so that you maintain and increase your career flexibility with every job you have.

Recent graduates considered career flexibility to be quite important to them. Among the most prevalent attributes of career flexibility, they identified several facets as most valuable.

Being qualified for more than one functional role. Being qualified for many roles encourages personal growth and allows survival in the corporate environment. As corporations downsize, eliminate middle management, and restructure, the easiest personnel to consider are those who are broadly capable. Often these are the individuals who are most apt to contribute to the restructuring plan and are given leadership responsibilities as well. From a defensive perspective, they are the least likely to be let go, because of their broad qualifications for other needs in the organization. They provide their employer's greater flexibility than other employees might.

Having broad responsibilities and experience. Closely related to the preceding, experiential breadth provides an organizational awareness that many employees fail to attain. The variety of tasks in a workday benefits from a range of responsibilities. This awareness allows one to recognize new opportunities within the organization more quickly and pursue them more effectively.

Having control over your career path. You do not want someone else in the driver's seat of your career. Having a sense of control, knowing that you can effect change when you need to, is critical to job satisfaction.

Being adaptable to people and situations. A number of respondents looked within when they volunteered the concept of adaptability. The flexibility of a career is often limited because the individual is inflexible and closed to changes occurring in his or her environment. Whether it is new management/supervision, different customers, a change in the design process, adaptability is key to maintaining a role within the organization.

Having a willingness to grow. Perhaps a form of intellectual curiosity, being open to new opportunities is important to the individual as well as the organization. In fact, willingness may be too passive a word. Many respondents might concur that a strong and active desire for growth will keep a job interesting and will continually provide new opportunities.

When asked to comment on career success, respondents wrote volumes. Summarized in Figure 2.2, a sampling of responses is listed here:

- *To me, a successful career means working in a field that is satisfying, with people whom you can grow with and enjoy, making enough money to lead the life you need, etc.*
- *A successful career is one in which you never "go to work."*
- *Success will come when a challenging career has been enjoyable. A career will fail to be a success if I know it could have existed without me!*
- *A successful career is founded on the growth of the individual, varied opportunities, travel, recognition, compensation, a feeling of contribution, and the ability to see readily impact of one's efforts on business success.*
- *Striving for excellence in everything . . . more attitudinal than hard-core results.*
- *Hard work + luck + ambition = success.*
- *Used to think it was a good salary and upward mobility. Now*

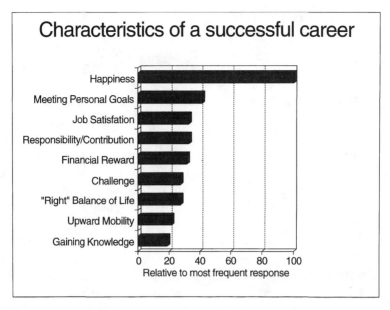

Figure 2.2   Characteristics of success

realize you need to be happy with your career and enjoy what you are doing.

If a definition of career success can be adopted that includes enjoyment, contribution, and flexibility, you will find that career objectives become much more attractive and, better yet, much more attainable. People who cling to money and position as the benchmarks are apt to consider their own careers incomplete or otherwise unsatisfactory. One may conclude that a realistic definition of success is a prerequisite for establishing career goals and objectives.

What Are Your Goals and Objectives?

College seniors have great difficulty in identifying and clarifying their career objectives. It isn't that seniors don't want to work or don't have a will to grow, they are simply entering a new environment. One common situation is when individuals have multiple interests—they want to do a lot of different things in their career, yet most entry-level positions offer relatively narrow responsibilities. It is reasonable to desire variety; in fact, most people will experience a number of changes in responsibility throughout their careers. Regardless, the individual's overriding interests must come into harmony with the opportunities at hand.

Everybody wants to be somebody; nobody wants to grow.
                                        Johann W. von Goethe

Naturally, when people have not developed an ability to articulate their personal objectives, it is highly unlikely that the objectives included on their résumé will be at all effective in the job search. This low effectiveness results from a lack of experience, from an unwillingness or inability to express themselves, and, perhaps, from the advice they are given for conducting their search. Expressed objectives are often overly general and ill defined. More than a few seniors, when pressed, will exclaim that the objectives presented in their résumés match those used by other students and seem to fit the general nature of what industry is looking for. Résumé objectives often have little to do with either what the individual or the prospective employer really wants. At the extreme, seniors refuse to consider their real career interests, and thus they cannot say much more to the recruiter than they want a job; certainly they are not prepared to discuss what employment possibilities might excite them. Needless to say, this is the wrong approach; and you should be able to do much better.

Whose career objective is it? Yours! It is difficult to set goals, particularly when so many others have advice for you. The avalanche of information available during the senior year can have a negative effect. One tends to rely on the array of information and advice provided and use canned approaches rather than personal judgment. The result is that stated career goals tend to regurgitate what the recruiters are expected to want to hear and overlook the applicant's personal desires for a career. Job hunters want to avoid the inclusion of any objective that might preclude an opportunity, so their objectives become vague and without direction. To the recruiter, these résumé objectives are, unfortunately, common. The recruiter has no idea what you really want, is not convinced that anything is actually exciting to you, and will not want to spend the time dragging it out of you.

Consider an alternative approach. Let us assume that there is a specific opportunity of interest to you. Given that this is the case, you probably have good reasons for your interest. These reasons are the foundation of your career objective. You may wish to refer to these as your real objectives. When I have been able to convince students to follow their hearts in this matter, their interviews have been much more effective. For one thing, less time was spent talking about opportunities that hold little interest. A much more important result is that the stated desire establishes a positive basis for the interview. Candor is greatly appreciated by prospective employers, and your enthusiasm will be attractive to the interviewer, even if your specified area of interest does not exactly fit his or her needs. If you can make that contact your advocate, he or she will inform you of other openings and opportunities existing, whether with that firm or elsewhere.

Does this pose a problem for you? No, it is an opportunity. Individuals are hired because people in the company like them. Of course, the company wants a logical basis for extending the offer. This logic is usually based upon education and experience deemed appropriate for the position, but logic is not enough. The decision to hire is an emotional one, first and foremost. Logic is important for meeting basic needs of the position, and it also is important to justify the decision already made for reasons of emotion. The prospective employer feels good about your attitude and is confident that you will get along well with the other employees—that you have a work ethic that will ensure you overcome any shortcomings in your education or experience.

So What Are the Objectives of an Objective?

These few words at the top of a résumé can accomplish miracles. Getting your objective(s) on paper in a fashion that is clear, accurate, and effective requires first that your own mind is clear—not as common as you might think. It also helps prospective employers to determine quickly if and why they want to consider you further.

Your objective is the most important writing you will do during your search, and if done properly, it ought to accomplish much. Does your objective meet the seven objectives listed below?

1. It is a rudder. It reminds you simply that you have a career direction in which you wish to proceed—it helps prevent you from getting confused.

2. It shows a prospective employer that you have direction and commitment. This, by the way, is exceptionally rare among all job applicants and college seniors in particular.

3. It demonstrates that your objective is reasonable and well suited to both you and the prospective employer.

4. It should demonstrate candor. The sooner that you can establish candor with a prospective employer, the more quickly the employer will accept the rest of your information as fact. At the risk of repeating myself, the importance of this point must be stressed. Far too many seniors play a word game in their search and fail to open up with either the recruiter or with themselves about their real career objectives.

5. It ought to project interest, resolve, and a positive attitude. Although few résumés accomplish this goal, it is not hard to do, and the results are quite remarkable.

6. It must be presented in a manner that is compatible with the recruiter's logical and emotional needs without surrendering any of your personal goals. This draws upon specific recruiting interests while maintaining your authenticity.

7. It should demonstrate your ability to think and to communicate well with management. What a wonderful accomplishment to be made by the time a prospective recruiter has read your first statement! If, in the space of two or three lines, you can accomplish these goals, then you communicate extremely well. If not, there are others who can. It appears that you have no choice but to learn to communicate extremely well. With written communications you can take as much time as you need to make an excellent presentation.

Take heart; just over one-third of the respondents indicated that they had established career goals when they graduated. After two or three years of experience, more than three-quarters had established definite career goals. For you, these statements mean that as you gain experience, you will become better able to determine what opportunities interest you the most. Recent graduates noted that work had allowed them to become more aware, more focused, and more realistic (Appendix A). It is not insignificant that the respondents, on average, reflected an increasing level of enthusiasm for their careers as they gained experience and awareness.

When asked what advice they might have to help college students establish career goals, many recent graduates volunteered their views. Among the most specific recommendations were to obtain as much career-related experience as possible through summer and cooperative work programs. These were the experiences that best helped the individual to set his or her course. In addition to experience, the value of researching companies carefully and making contacts in the individual's area of interest also is strongly recommended. This allows the applicant access to information going well beyond that provided during the interview. Companies are impressed with candidates who have done their homework.

Among the more personal recommendations were to not fear change but maintain an open mind regarding opportunities. In addition to specific recommendations, a number of comments were volunteered. Some are provided here:

- *Analyze your strengths and weaknesses to find a good match for your values and personality; then compare that result to positions available in the job market. Professional work experience as an undergraduate is a great way to test potential pursuits.*

- *Take a broad range of courses to start seeking to expose yourselves to as broad a spectrum of possible paths. If something seems interesting, pursue it. If not, keep looking. Research the companies. Big companies are impersonal but usually more stable. Smaller companies and younger companies are more intimate but less secure. Think about it.*

- *Talk to people in all aspects of a company; do not focus yourself so early. A career path does not need to be a straight line; lateral experience is rare and rewarding. Be honest with yourself and be flexible.*

- *Picture where you want to be in five years and what you want to be doing. Then base all your life decisions on getting to that point.*

- *Start with something that interests you. You don't have to plan your whole career before it starts. Enjoy the time you have and learn about yourself.*

Establishing and expressing a clear objective is the first critical step in building your career. Do effective managers and leaders work without clear objectives? Absolutely not. In the next section, we will look at the job search. As we turn to the résumé, your objective will be the grand opening. If it is to be a forthright objective that demonstrates your candor, it may well be the one aspect of your résumé written in the first person.

Senior Housekeeping

In order to get a few details out of the way prior to proceeding with the job search, a few important topics are mentioned. These are relevant to a successful search effort, yet often pose difficulty.

Dress. It is important to dress appropriately—good choice of colors, good fit, and conservatively. Well-pressed clothes, shined shoes, and carefully groomed hair reflect care on the part of the individual. They are not enough to win the job, but they can be a factor that removes you from consideration.

Conversation. Tend to keep conversation formal rather than casual. Swearing, use of slang, and grammatical errors reflect a lack of taste, education, or both. Above all else, conversation must be honest and deliberate. The most common pitfall is to overanalyze what you are going to say to the point that you appear distant or indirect. Earl Nightingale (1986) notes that when you meet other people, they will probably form an opinion about your education and intelligence by the time you have completed your first sentence. You may do the same about others. Whether it is conversation or the start of your résumé, find out how others perceive you and consider how you want them to perceive you.

Hygiene. People are too gentle with each other. Students can live among school friends for four years and still not be told that they have bad breath or strong body odor. It is hard to confront others with these issues, but overlooking them does a friend no good.

How prevalent are these problems? My guess is that one in ten students has a problem without realizing it. If this is a possibility with you, find someone who will tell you the truth, and, if necessary, find a way to control it. To put it in other terms, if I were interviewing for a position and you had this kind of problem, it might well preclude you from further consideration, and I would not be likely to tell you why.

Attitude. Your attitude is critical to your success. Recruiters will often overlook deficits in the desired education or experience if they perceive a positive attitude. On the other hand, a candidate with excellent education and experience who shows a poor attitude is a terrible risk. Again referring to Earl Nightingale, people with good attitudes get hired and receive promotions; people with poor attitudes do not. The nice thing is that only you are responsible for your attitude—not your parents, not your adviser, not your supervisor/manager, and not your friends. Only you can determine if it will work for you or against you.

The 4.0 student. It is not unusual for a student to perform exceptionally well in his or her academic program and then experience considerable difficulty in the job search. There may be several reasons for this, but the most likely is that this student has learned the rules and discipline for performing well in school but does not yet understand the importance of feedback from others. This is, of course, disastrous in the interview and throughout the search.

Two recommendations for the outstanding student are first, make certain that you are an effective listener and second, recognize that the decision processes leading to your next employment opportunity go well beyond the logic of education and accomplishment.

Workload. Many students have stated that the senior search effort requires more attention than most courses. The senior year is an exciting one, but it is also a stressful one. The demands for balancing interviews and job-search trips with classes and exams are shared by all students who seek to complete a successful education and commence a successful career.

Elective courses. In the previously mentioned survey of recent graduates, several additional recommendations were offered for college seniors. Because they are early in their careers, and presumably their college experiences are still fresh in their minds, their thoughts and recommendations are worth noting. The general finding of this survey was that these recent graduates were enthusiastic about their careers, and they were giving the merits of their education careful consideration.

A variety of views was offered regarding the selection of elective course work. I would expect that specific recommendations correlate closely with functional job responsibilities, although the survey data did not accommodate that kind of analysis. The recommendations were in response to open-ended questions, and the top six areas for recommended electives included communications (42 percent of all respondents), engineering (40 percent), management (39 percent), marketing (38 percent), information systems (24 percent), and the liberal arts (8 percent). The selection of electives can help an individual develop depth, develop breadth, or pursue interests.

The Two Sides of Stress

It has been said that looking for a job is the toughest job there is. Beginning with the senior year, you encounter a whole new range of stresses. This is the start of the process of building a career. To say that it is not easy in no way means that careers cannot be enjoyable or fulfilling. It is exactly the stresses encountered with new situations that force you to reflect, cope, and grow.

One aspect of a successful career is to pursue the difficult tasks in order to gain the opportunities they eventually present. It is a hard lesson to teach because it is not a part of the educational structure. As you face one challenge after another, you will come to better realize the abilities you have for growth and con-

tribution. The topic of stress is encountered again in Chapter 4.
With a discussion of students and education now behind us,
our attention is drawn to the search, the career, and leadership.

Chapter 3

You—A Functional Perspective

When you get right down to the
meaning of the word "succeed,"
you find that it simply means
to follow through.

F. W. Nichol

The Importance of Your Résumé

This chapter includes an emphasis on résumé preparation and is intended to assist college seniors in their search efforts by promoting an increased awareness of industrial perspectives. I believe that extensive examples are worthwhile in helping seniors; experienced individuals may prefer to skim the contents of this chapter. However, a large number of examples exposes the individual piecemeal to some values of free enterprise in a manner to which he or she can relate.

If you can land the job you want, you probably have the abilities to excel in that job once you get it. After all, the processes and attitudes required for landing your first job are not so different from those that lead to increased opportunities and promotion. Such is the pathway of career growth. Consider that an established career objective, an implemented plan, an awareness of business needs, and marshalled communication skills are all prerequisites for conducting a successful search.

This coordination of effort is just as effective in pursuing increased responsibility. Yet, once a position is obtained, it is natural for a new hire to turn his or her attention to the details of the new job and abandon the broad business awareness, planning, and careful communications that contributed so greatly to the success of the search. New hires become shortsighted by adopting a narrow view of their responsibilities and the business needs around them.

Carefully consider, on personal terms, the successful job search process, even though you may already be happily employed. Even if you have risen to a level of significant managerial responsibilities, the effective career search effort offers an excellent model for maintaining an effective relationship throughout your career. This model will work for you and for all who are under your supervision. This chapter isn't really about finding a job; it is about working well with people. These challenges are not so different, regardless of whether you are working with subordinates, superiors, or potential employers.

To involve others effectively, the effective job search requires the candidate first to have his or her own house in order. This goal involves career direction, realistic self-image, a sense of personal values, confidence, and assertiveness. The criteria for a successful search seem obvious. Yet often these are ignored and the job search fails. Criteria for a successful search include the following:

1. *A career objective that is heartfelt and well articulated.* It is difficult for college seniors to construct an appropriate and effective career objectives due to their lack of exposure. Although career goals become clearer as experience is gained, the catch is this: It is hard to obtain a job without clear objectives, and it is equally difficult to establish meaningful career objectives without the benefit of experience. As a college senior, you have no choice but to develop your career objective. The sooner you do, the more quickly you can overcome the dilemma of no job.

   Although your objective must be well articulated, it is much more than a few words on paper. Above all, it must be something that you believe in and for which you are willing to sacrifice. Employers will look to see the extent that stated objectives parallel your interests and passions. In other words, tell the recruiter what you really like; do not strive to tell them only what you think they want to hear. They will know the difference immediately.

Your objective must be readable, understandable, rational, and agreeable. Even so, it must also be immediately to the point.

2. *Awareness of personal interests, strengths, and weaknesses.* Applicants commonly fail to understand how well suited their interests, experience, and education may be for a particular job opportunity. Your background of education and experience can provide the best justification for your career objectives.

I have frequently seen students overlook important attributes such as being multilingual, paying their own way through school, starting a successful summer business, or performing volunteer services. It is particularly difficult for college seniors to relate the merits of their work experience, albeit limited, to the needs of companies recruiting on campus. For example, one individual indicated on his résumé that he drove a truck and forklift at a lumber yard but overlooked the role he assumed in working well with customers. He was excellent in resolving customer problems and complaints, and many customers came to prefer him as their point of contact. He had a measurable positive impact on total sales, yet this had not been apparent in his résumé or during his interviews unless someone accidentally found out about these "other" responsibilities he had assumed!

Once the senior saw the relevance of his customer service experience and gave it appropriate attention on his résumé, he became much more confident in his interviews. He was convinced of the importance of this additional information and brought it up during interviews. Through this process he came to a clearer understanding of the business world so that he could better relate to their needs.

This case demonstrates how unrecognized accomplishments can relate directly to the needs of industry, such accomplishments can provide a most effective way for the candidate to project a positive attitude.

Likewise, personal interests can be strongly related to employment opportunities and used to the applicant's advantage. A young woman I know performs most of the maintenance and repair work on her mother's car. The extent of her work includes brake replacement and body repair as well as tune-ups and oil changes. She also has the experience of rebuilding an engine. She told me she worked on cars for two reasons: First, she and her mother did not always have the money to spend at a garage and second, she enjoys it. She is seeking a hands-on opportunity in industry in the area of manufacturing or testing. Clearly, her interests and experience relate well with her career objective, and recruiters will like this a lot.

People have shortcomings and aversions as well. It is important that applicants be aware of and be able to discuss any point that may concern a recruiter. You may be uneasy about meeting new people, working in large groups, and giving presentations. Some of these fears will be overcome over the course of your career, but it does not sound as if you would be comfortable in a sales job. When you discuss your objectives, you should be able to offer good supporting logic based upon your strengths. Do not base your objective upon negative logic, i.e., "I know one thing, I sure don't want to sit at a desk all day." Your shortcomings are apt to become a topic of conversation during the interview. Be able to acknowledge them and discuss them *briefly* without being defensive. Be prepared to turn the conversation toward your strengths, your interests, and/or your accomplishments. Let the interviewer know that you have full confidence that your objectives are fully compatible with your strengths as well as your weaknesses.

3. *Awareness of needs and opportunities in industry.* Good job opportunities continually arise and disappear. In a slow job market, they are somewhat less frequent, they are filled a little more quickly, and more people apply for the opportunity, but those are really the only differences.

The decision processes and criteria do not change. Regardless of the market, employers will want to have the important positions filled as quickly as possible. Thus, the successful applicant is forced to maintain an awareness of new openings in sufficient time to assess the opportunity, collect additional information, and act.

I'M PLEASED TO TELL YOU THAT MY CAREER GOALS ARE CRYSTAL CLEAR - IN THE FIRST TWO YEARS I WANT TO GAIN SIGNIFICANT INDUSTRIAL AND MANAGERIAL EXPERIENCE; THEN I PLAN TO RETURN HOME TO RUN DAD'S BUSINESS.

To capitalize on these opportunities, an applicant must come to know the industry and a company well enough to be attuned to an employer's needs. This, of course, dictates that the applicant must go well beyond the knowledge that a position exists and what it entails. The only way an applicant will get a job, however, is by meeting the needs of an employer. When the candidate has familiarity with market issues, regulatory challenges, or company heritage, for example, he or she is likely to have a much better sensitivity for the employer's greatest concerns. These concerns or needs are generally not identified in the job posting.

You can get everything in life you want . . . If you'll just help enough other people get what they want.

Zig Ziglar

4. *Ability and desire to communicate effectively.* Communications skills are carefully observed by college recruiters with good reason: Communication problems represent a needless expense of time and effort for the organization. Employees may be paid to solve engineering and project management problems but not to solve problems created internally. Inability to write or speak well is held up as a common complaint regarding new hires, and the ability to communicate is probably the most readily assessed characteristic during the interview. An applicant's success is predicated upon his or her ability to convincingly articulate experience, education, skills, and goals.

Possession of the right qualifications has little value to a candidate when a recruiter remains unaware of such experience, abilities, and accomplishments. As you learn how to establish your communications skills with prospective employers, you will see them gain confidence in your ability to function satisfactorily within their organization.

5. *Attitude: your visible resolve to learn, work, and contribute.* With so many qualified applicants to choose from, why bother hiring an individual who does not present a positive attitude? Possessing and projecting the right attitude can often overcome deficiencies the recruiter may see in your education or experience.

Turning toward the career search, the student encounters a completely different environment, which operates under a whole new set of rules. Effort and outcomes vary considerably among graduating seniors. Certainly, the transition to career is satisfactorily started when all the criteria above have been satisfied.

As a starting point of the search process, consider your résumé. I have held three distinctly different views over the years regarding the role of a résumé in a job search. Initially, it seemed to me that a résumé was the critical component of a successful search. I supposed that if the résumé were well enough prepared, it could land almost any job. My focus was on the piece of paper and how it might motivate some captain of industry to give me a great job.

Of course, I was wrong. At that time, I had no real idea that employers needed far more than a set of stated credentials on a piece of paper. As my career progressed, my views regarding the résumé shifted significantly. I saw that almost anyone could come up with a fairly good résumé, but such seemed the domain of impostors. It seemed to me that true engineers were too busy doing good work to generate a fancy document of fluff. To me, the true ability for an individual to deliver was far more important than facility for projecting an image of ability. I wondered if ability and image had become inversely related on the résumés we were receiving. At this point, I felt that résumés had become far overrated; they seemed little more than pieces of paper that, more often than not, got in the way of real communications among the employer and applicant. Frequently, job candidates would use a résumé as a conversation crutch during the interview, thus declining to speak from their hearts about career ambitions. This tended to be my view after I assumed increasing management responsibilities, and, in retrospect, this view has an element of truth. As a piece of paper, the value of a résumé for finding the right job seemed truly overrated. Almost all résumés attempt to project an image and fail to project the person.

To be persuasive we must be believable, / To be believable, we must be credible, / To be credible we must be truthful.

Edward R. Murrow

As my responsibilities evolved toward teaching, advising, and career placement, my views regarding the role of a résumé changed again. The crafting of an outstanding résumé is the single most important step undertaken in a career search. Its value cannot be overstated. What the résumé offers the applicant is a process, not a piece of paper. The creation of an excellent functional résumé forces the individual to identify and clearly describe accomplishments, interests, and goals—no small feat!

The effort of constructing such a document will help you better understand the needs of prospective employers. Once the important elements are on paper, considerable work is required to make it useful to recruiters. The applicant must reflect on what recruiters want, how they think, and how they make decisions. At this point, an applicant is starting to learn a lot about industry and management; it is time very well spent.

Unfortunately, most résumés have been butchered. One reason is that there are too many poor examples to follow. Many books on job hunting and résumé preparation are written by people who have never participated significantly in the staffing and management of an organization. Another reason is that students approach a job search like a college course. They follow guidelines and expect the averages of continued success to continue in their favor. Students seldom attempt to complete much more than minimum requirements for a course—the differences in student grades are based upon how these minimums are met. Following the same approach, students often fail to put appropriate care into the search effort, and it is too late when they finally determine that their effort is unsuccessful. I believe that most of the people who can offer good advice regarding a career development strategy are too busy running their own organizations.

RULE 1: Promote the Person, not the Image.
RULE 2: Start with Your Résumé.

Paul Sorbo was a senior who was enjoyable to work with. He was a fairly good student who made the dean's list several times, yet he was also a down-to-earth kind of individual. He was active in his fraternity and enjoyed a good time but also worked hard to pay his way through a private university. Paul enjoyed music and would travel great distances to see rock concerts. He had been a star hockey player in high school with opportunities to play Division I hockey in college. He felt that sports at that level would impede his ability to balance social interests with academic responsibilities. In college he was diligent in pursuing his education and career.

Paul had worked at a bicycle shop from the age of twelve through high school and college. In this job, Paul had been given increasing responsibilities over the years, which included computerizing the bookkeeping, training new employees, new promotional initiatives, and expanding services and the range of product lines. He had held a few other odd jobs as well, but nothing that seemed to relate to his career goals. Paul had not found a co-op opportunity in industry like many had. He had conducted several interviews and had also taken the time to talk with recent alums about his career goals. He was thinking that he liked engineering, but he did not want to go into design as many of his classmates were. Paul liked commerce and wanted an opportunity to work with customers as well as technology.

Out of concern, Paul came to see me about his job search. There were interesting opportunities out there, but he had not made significant progress. We met for about forty-five minutes to discuss his interests and look at his resume. During that meeting, I put Paul under some stress with my questioning and suggested that his résumé was almost useless. His search strategy did not take advantage of his strengths, and I felt that he would probably not find the position he was looking for. It was a negative picture for Paul, but I also showed him how he might overcome the hurdles he currently faced by using a change in his approach. Paul left my office determined to get to the bottom of his problems, but he was not yet sure whether my advice was helpful or harmful.

Over the course of two weeks, we met three more times to discuss his résumé and search effort. Through these discussions, Paul was better able to sort out his capabilities, wants, and accomplishments. The task of preparing a more effective and accurate résumé helped Paul clarify his career goals and realign his strategy. It was a process of maturation that provided Paul with more than a piece of paper; it gave him the direction and confidence necessary for completing his search successfully.

Anyone aspiring to career growth in industry, whether job-hunting or not, should update his or her résumé regularly. There are several excellent formats to consider in preparing an effective résumé, but I strongly recommend starting with a modified approach to preparing a functional résumé (FR). This approach, discussed in detail, offers the most direct approach for candidates to use in addressing their qualities as they relate to the needs of industry. Once the FR is complete, you may decide to use another format for utilizing the information your FR has helped you to assemble. It is also possible that your FR accomplishes exactly what you want it to.

An extensive assortment of information is available regarding the job search, which this book does not seek to replicate. Unfortunately, the majority of published resources I have seen regarding job hunting, resume building, and letter writing may do more harm than good. As previously indicated, I feel that the central problem is that much of the available literature is written by individuals who are outside of the decision processes. They have neither hired nor managed professional people in industry and, therefore, do not have first-hand experience with business hiring rationale.

There are, of course, excellent resources available as well.

Bolles' *What Color is Your Parachute?* (1994) is a well respected resource that is revised annually. It is designed for a general audience and does not address many of the needs that may be specific to engineers. It does a good job of covering topics such as career planning, résumés, strategies, networking, and career changes. One of my favorite parts, included as an epilogue, is "How to Find Your Mission in Life." It may be the best general resource available for helping the individual with his or her career planning. Asher has written three excellent books—one on the transition from college to career (1992), another on changing jobs, and one on résumé writing (1991). Again, these books are not targeted at the professions, but I believe the information content is excellent. Professional societies have necessarily taken an increasingly active role in providing their membership with career related information and resources. In my opinion, IEEE's U.S. Activities Board has compiled several excellent resources specifically for engineers. One resource, edited by Backe (1991) is quite helpful. Appendix B provides a list and comments on these and many other available materials relevant to your career pursuits.

Although this chapter addresses the search effort, its emphasis is clearly on the résumé, for two reasons. First, you need to have a document that represents you well. Although it is my opinion that most of the available advice regarding résumé preparation is counterproductive, you can construct a document that will work effectively for you. The second—and more important—reason is the process of self-evaluation you need to experience as you consolidate your history and hopes onto a single page of paper. Use this effort to contemplate the needs of prospective employers. In doing so, the modified FR process will help you clarify your best attributes in your own mind as well as for the prospective employer.

The Functional Résumé

To treat your facts with imagination is one thing,
but to imagine your facts is another.
                                        John Burroughs

This single sheet of paper has many purposes that you must recognize. Your ability to meet the objectives of the résumé will determine the extent to which it can work to your favor. Students have indicated that once they have rethought their résumé using some of the suggestions given here, they were much more effective in expressing their goals and gaining significant career opportunities. Not only that, they felt much more optimistic that their career was going to be fun!

From your perspective, the modified FR process may only add to the range of conflicting and confusing information that you already have considered. Consider this: Given that the modified FR process may be either right or wrong, it is up to you alone to consider all the alternatives and select the best game plan. There is an elegance in this responsibility because you are the one who needs the job, and you are the one who suffers if you fail at your search. Fortunately, you are also the one to benefit when you meet with success. The point is this: You cannot get what you want until you do it right, and that means you have to know which approach will work best for you. You can figure that out now, or you can bounce around awhile until you find an approach that does work. Welcome to the world of industry—when you do the job right, doors open!

After the modified FR is complete, consider the merits of other styles and approaches. You may wish to keep your FR as is, or you may select another format to submit to potential employers. They can tell you best their perceptions of its positive and negative attributes. Let's get on with it.

Who Reads Your Résumé?

Your résumé is prepared for the purpose of helping an employer match his or her needs with your abilities, yet your résumé must be unique. Given that millions of people in the United States each may send out hundreds of résumés annually and also that most résumés fail in their mission, résumé readers become conditioned to not expect much. They have access to more résumés than they want (quantity, not quality), so they become impatient and tired. Very few will read your entire résumé. Your parents might read it, and perhaps a few others who have time on their hands but no authority to offer you the job opportunity you want will look at it. However, very few people who can help you will read it. If you are conducting interviews on a college campus, it will be reviewed quickly by your interviewer. If you are mailing résumés, you will be lucky if 5 percent of the content is read.

If those who need to hire someone like you only read a small part of your résumé, shouldn't you think about what they want to read and where they will look for it? You have to know what information is important to the employer and how to make that information prominent. In this manner, you can help them to relate their needs to your attributes.

> *A page of history is worth a pound of logic.*
> Oliver Wendell Holmes, Jr.

Recruiters follow a pattern when they read a résumé. First they look at the objective to determine the relevance of the applicant's interests with their recruiting needs. If the objective fails to match, the recruiter will remove the candidate from further consideration and move along to the next applicant. Likewise, if the objective is vague and lacks resolve, the recruiter will fail to see a match and will go on to the next candidate, hoping to at last find a match.

When a career objective is compatible with a position, the recruiter will read further, looking quickly for additional relevant information. Figure 3.1 is a map showing the premium real estate on your resume. Recruiters look for key words to help them decide whether your application should be passed on to the operating group for consideration. Through key words, they want to determine quickly if you have the right experience, education, and attitude to meet their needs. Where do the key words go? They belong in your premium real estate. They help the reader decide whether the rest of the line will be a waste of time. Contrary to popular advice, action verbs are often poor key words. How does a person project attitude on paper? It is not hard, but I am surprised each time I see it done well. We get to attitude later.

It is interesting to note that the words on your résumé that are the most beautiful and have the most prominent size and location are the last ones read—your name. These words hold no useful information until the recruiter has determined that you meet enough criteria for them to want to meet with you. Even

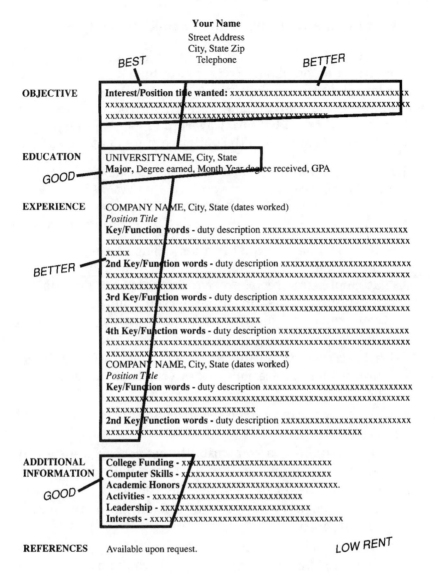

Figure 3.1. Premium Résumé Real Estate.

your home address offers more useful information than your name—it tells a prospective employer whether they will have to pay relocation expenses or not. What then should be done with a résumé if the reader does not even care about your name?

What Are the Goals of a Functional Résumé?

Believe it or not, there are more than a dozen goals that a résumé should accomplish. Some relate to you, the applicant; some relate to the individual in HR who screens résumés; and some relate to the individual(s) with whom you hope to interview. You will note substantial overlap among the respective missions of your resume and the objective statement it contains.

When I am working on a problem, I never think about beauty.
I think only how to solve the problem. But when I have
finished, if the solution is not beautiful, I know it is wrong.

Buckminster Fuller

Goal 1. Define your qualifications. The process of preparing a good FR will help you view your accomplishments, attributes, interests, and career goals from an industry perspective. This will encourage you to have greater self-confidence and motivation for completing a successful search.

Goal 2. Project your career direction. The FR should clearly present your professional objective(s) to potential employers.

Goal 3. Sensitize yourself to the perspectives and needs of employers.

Goal 4. Establish a compatibility between you and your prospective employer. It relates your abilities, objective, education, and experience to their needs.

Goal 5. Demonstrate your professional maturity and career stability.

Goal 6. Project confidence and reason. This can be effectively accomplished in your objective statement, but look for other opportunities to send this message in a subtle, but effective, manner.

Goal 7. Provide a clear example of your excellent business communication skills. However, do not state that you have good communications skills. Show them instead, and let them draw that conclusion. See Goal 11.

Goal 8. Demonstrate respect for management. Information

is presented in management's terms and is organized to save management's time and effort. Nothing extraneous is included.

Goal 9.   Project your enthusiasm and positive attitude (this complements Goal 6). Few people accomplish this at all, and when they do, it is often during an interview. It is also possible to accomplish this on your résumé. See Goal 11.

Goal 10. Provide a clear example of diligence and perfection. A résumé is one of the few business communications in which you have the opportunity to use as much time and effort as is necessary to do the job exactly right.

Goal 11. Present facts, not judgments. Statements such as "I developed good communications skills" are almost as bad "I am good looking." Self-evaluations can make you appear defensive, self-centered, or insincere. Avoid them, and others will be more likely to believe you.

Goal 12. Establish your uniqueness. It is natural for seniors and recent graduates to desire association with the right crowd. For instance, you might have an engineering degree and an MBA degree, yet there are a multitude of individuals with exactly these same qualifications. By the time the employer gets to the decision time for extending an offer, he or she has to understand how you are different (better) and not the same as every other application.

Goal 13. Establish candor by presenting yourself as a person and not a position. It helps the reader understand your motivations as well as your accomplishments and goals.

Goal 14. Provide an agenda for the interview. Topics you wish to discuss are highlighted on the résumé, and you have included comments that invite questions you enjoy addressing. A well-phrased résumé, when used as the interview agenda, promotes optimism and confidence.

This is a tall order for a single page of text, but your résumé can accomplish every one of these goals. In fact, a good résumé accomplishes these goals in less space than is required to list them! Does your current résumé accomplish these goals? How do you know?

To draw upon a concept used in sociology, your resume can function as a mirror, a mask, or a window. Many job applicants are drawn to the mask and the mirror because the window scares them, yet only the window works.

Mirror. When an applicant uses an overly general objective, one that fails to identify specific career direction, he or she is trying to keep open all possible job opportunities. One recruiter expresses a need for manufacturing personnel; another needs marketing people; and yet another wants designer engineers. Because the candidate wants each recruiter to find something different, the résumé acts as a mirror to reflect the recruiter's interests.

The mirror fails to work well because recruiters look for specific direction and for motivation. The mirror fails in its mission because it projects neither of these characteristics but is instead perceived as uncertainty or lack of drive.

Mask. It is natural that college seniors choose a general career direction because many opportunities exist in that field. Sometimes these opportunities coincide well with the applicant's interests, but often seniors have not resolved what they really want from in their career. Others may have specific interests but deny them. Why? They may not see that opportunities exist that align well with their interests, or perhaps the thought of working for a name company seems more important than going for the position that better suits their functional interests. Often, individuals pursue interviews on campus only because the opportunity exists to interview. Senior engineering students who wish to work in design will likely perform poorly in an interview for a marketing position.

People from all walks of life write objectives that make quality improvement seem like their lifelong ambition only because there is a job opening, and they want a job. These résumés are a mask, and they do not work; in fact, they are less effective than the mirror. An interviewer will recognize your lack of commitment within the first minute of the interview, from that point on, he or she will view the interview as a waste of his or her time.

Window. The most effective approach is to use your résumé as an instrument for recruiters to get to know you as an individual—a window for them to use in gaining a sense of your attitudes, thinking, and motivations. You have an opportunity to insert your interests and more personal information among the facts in ways that support your objectives and complement your accomplishments. If, for example, volunteer service is an important part of your life, it may be worth mentioning on your résumé in the space of a few words. On the other hand, do not say that volunteer work is central to your spare time if it is not—you will have turned your window into a mask, and the recruiter will be on to the next application.

RULE 3: Always Be Honest.

What Are the Components of a Functional Résumé?

A simple approach is preferred in categorizing the information on the FR. Your address and telephone number are usually under your name at the top if you are job hunting. If your résumé is for use at work, perhaps to be included with a group of résumés appended to a business proposal, then a *Personal Statement* or *Summary Statement* is more appropriate than an objective. *Career Objective* will be the first order of business with recruiters, so put it at the top, under your name. The remaining categories include *Experience, Education*, and *Additional Information*. For college seniors, educational information includes the most relevant information; thus, it follows the objective. Once you have acquired sufficient experience, education moves downward on the FR, and experience is placed directly under the objective. Experience probably should not be split into subcategories such as *Professional Experience, Part-Time Work*, and *Other Experience*. When too many headings are used, a résumé becomes cluttered, thus confusing the recruiter. Recruiters stop reading when they get lost or confused.

Objective

It was mentioned earlier that recruiters look at objectives first, which is not exactly true. Recruiters read the first several words of the objective and decide whether to continue. The objective can actually be quite long (three or four lines), but the first one, two, or three words ought to commit to a career objective. The remainder of your objective statement can include a justification for your career goals. Readers need to know immediately whether or not you may be suited for their recruiting needs, so opening phrases such as "A position that . . . " or "I am seeking a position in . . . " work against you. There is no need to state that you are seeking a position; do not waste the most valuable space on your résumé. A well-written objective will accomplish many goals, but you must believe in it. It is the only way you can get someone else to believe you.

> *Anytime you don't want anything, you get it.*
> Calvin Coolidge

One way to get attention is to hit hard with the first one or two words of the resume. If you want to design circuits, perhaps circuit design ought to be the opening words of your objective statement. This demonstrates focus and commitment, and already you have differentiated yourself from most applicants. Seniors have difficulty committing, even when circuit design is exactly what they want. If, after this opening, the recruiter is still reading your resume, she may be looking at the right person, and you may be looking at the right employer. A two-word objective may not accomplish all the goals set out in Chapter 2, but it can be highly effective.

The applicant benefits by having a direction that can be expressed in four words or less. First, brevity demands that you commit to a direction. Do not overlook the importance of this. It is one way to force you to say what you want, rather than what you believe others will want to hear. Also, it may be your first attempt at getting to the point. I recommend strongly against writing different objectives for each prospective opportunity. It is a quick way to forget what you want from your career.

If the objective statement can be up to four lines long, but you have stated your goal in the first several words, think of what you can accomplish with the remainder of your objective statement! If the recruiter is still reading, you know that a compatibility of functional interests exists. What might recruiters want to know next about you? They want to see that you have good justification for this goal. They want to see a positive attitude toward work. They will be pleased if they sense you are being honest with them. And they will be attracted to those who express themselves effectively. Several examples, both good and bad, are listed here for your consideration:

Poor Examples

A challenging position in the field of electrical engineering optimizing my problem-solving skills and education.

To obtain a position allowing me to use my technical skills with software and hardware in a team-oriented environment.

A challenging position involving engineering-related work that will utilize my interests and experience.

To gain employment in a stimulating environment using both technical and practical experiences.

A challenging position in manufacturing or sales that will utilize and enhance my education and interpersonal skills.

To acquire a challenging position that would allow me to grow and assume management responsibilities.

To obtain a position enhancing my electrical engineering education by combining my thorough problem-solving skills and knowledge of electrical systems analysis.

More Effective Examples

Quality Improvement / Manufacturing: I enjoyed the challenging responsibilities of quality control at Big Three Automobile Company and saw that I could make a measurable contribution to operational performance through quality improvement. This experience has confirmed my desire to improve quality in a manufacturing environment.

Manufacturing: A position requiring technical and analytical competence, with opportunities for becoming an effective leader. The ideal organization must be committed to total quality and stress effective communications, leadership, and self-motivation.

Electrical Design and Testing—Power Systems: I enjoy analyzing and solving production related problems in a team environment. The ideal opportunity will be with a utility or architect/engineering firm with activities in plant modifications, repair, or start-up.

Manufacturing: I enjoy working with people, solving technical problems, and improving manufacturing processes. Ten years of industrial experience have taught me that a team approach to continuous improvement increases productivity and job satisfaction.

Project Management: Planning, scheduling, and contract administration associated with large-scale projects. I enjoy the challenge of balancing the needs of trade supervision with the objectives of plant management in a competitive environment.

Application Engineer: I enjoy interacting with customers and designing products to fit their individual needs and specifications. My professional experience in power transmission has offered an excellent opportunity for me to work in a highly competitive environment that demanded effective teamwork.

In writing your objective it is necessary for you first to consider your own desires and expectations. Although the topic at hand is your résumé, the greater task is defining the characteristics of a position that match your personal preferences. Career-development offices, employment agencies, and recruiters will tend to focus the conversation on functional titles. This is natural on their part but can be difficult for you. There are ways to present your objectives that will promote your interests while encouraging a match with an employer's needs.

Personal/Summary Statement

The individual has flexibility in forming a personal statement. Rather than what you want, it emphasizes what you do and what you have accomplished. It is an important statement, and all the objective statement goals listed in Chapter 2 should be considered when preparing an opening résumé statement.

Education

For a senior or recent graduate, education is most important because that may be all there is! As the individual gains experience, the importance of information regarding education diminishes quickly. Education includes college degrees earned and can include grade-point average, academic honors, significant projects, and selected course concentrations. Emphasis on education can signal a lack of experience. If you include course work or project discussion, it should visibly relate to the objective. Such information should be brief and to the point. Examples are provided in the section titled "Additional Information." In general, information regarding high school education should not be included.

If you have completed graduate work and your thesis topic relates to your career objective, it can be mentioned here. Assuming that graduate work is related to the career, key words should be highlighted in bold, italics, or with underlining. Do not try to make the readers understand the details of your research. The more briefly you present information, the more likely it is that they will be able to read it. The more enthusiasm you can project, the more they will like it.

In general, recent graduates should include grade-point average. If your average increased significantly during your final three or four semesters, calculate and list your academic average for that period of time as well. Many recruiters can tolerate average or below-average academic performance if they see justification or evidence of improvement.

After your first professional job, education should be placed somewhere after experience. Placing education at the top shows its importance to you, but it also flags you as inexperienced. Some students have had significant experience with prior work, co-op positions, or family businesses. They may consider placing this experience ahead of education if it relates well to their career objective. Donald Asher notes that the degree has a short half-life (1992): that the "graduate only has one or two years to sell her education before her 'real world' experience becomes the (overwhelmingly) dominant factor. . . ."

Finally, with regard to education, many résumés have the name of the university in bold. However, it may be more relevant to place emphasis on electrical engineering and master of business administration if those are your degree areas.

I have never let my schooling interfere with my education.
Mark Twain

Experience

Two individuals can view the same work responsibilities in completely different ways—which is often the case when one individual is seasoned in industry and the other is not. For this reason, work experience is sometimes more relevant than what the applicant projects on the résumé or in the interview. The applicant may focus on the equipment and software used, whereas the recruiter is interested in the applicant's motivation and effectiveness when working with others.

Recent graduates will sometimes categorize experience as "professional" and "other" to highlight their best career-related experiences. This approach has merit when the competition is only other college seniors. The drawback is that it reminds the recruiter that much of the experience is not professional and is probably not related to the job. Let's face it; you are a greenhorn, and you look like one! Consider limiting your résumé to one category of experience, and include all experience that relates to your career objective.

It is not necessary to detail on your résumé all positions you have held, particularly those part-time jobs that may have helped pay college expenses but provided no relevant experience. If you have held a number of part-time and temporary positions, such as answering telephones, tending bar, or working at the towel room in the gym, a simple statement referring to the miscellaneous other responsibilities you have held to defray college expenses may be sufficient. A recruiter who desires the names, addresses, and dates of employment for these odd jobs will ask you for it. Avoiding this detailed information on your résumé allows you to emphasize your most relevant experience.

If possible, place your most relevant experience and best accomplishments at the top of your experience section. Experience need not be chronological, but make sure you do not look like you are hiding periods of unemployment or other problems. One approach is to list employers, titles, and dates in order but save the explanation of functional responsibilities for a later section.

YEAH, I USED TO HAVE A HELL OF A TIME WITH THE ENGLISH LANGUAGE!

On the sample résumés you will see several ideas for presenting your work experience. Various font styles are available for emphasizing key words while maintaining an attractive and readable format. Under experience, you may emphasize the company name in bold or capital letters, yet your responsibilities and accomplishments are much more appropriate for highlighting. For example, you may have worked for several organizations that the recruiter has never heard of, and you may have held the title of summer help. There is nothing in this information deserving emphasis on your résumé. You may have had responsibilities that allowed you to make important contributions to the business or that helped you to develop your career-related interests and abilities. Isn't this where the emphasis should be? For this reason, I am a strong advocate of presenting experience in short statements under topical headings. The information is about you, and the topics relate it to the recruiter's needs. Thus, the topics are signposts for the recruiter.

When recruiters see a topic such as manufacturing, design, construction, or supervision in bold, they can determine immediately if they should read that line further. What you place after the topic should summarize what you did that highlights your contribution to the business. Accomplishments such as increased sales, reduced scrap, and decreased inventory levels are valuable. Make sure that you select topics that relate to the recruiter's interests. By following this approach, you demonstrate your sensitivity to the company's business issues.

The use of action verbs is commonly advised, yet such verbs seldom have strong impact. Students will start sentences with words such as handled, delivered, wrapped, or observed, but these words offer no incentive for the recruiter to read further. In fact, a child could compose a résumé using many of the same action verbs you might select. You will be fortunate if a recruiter reads more than one word in ten of your résumé. Therefore, your challenge is to focus on topics of interest to the recruiters. The categorization of your experience will ensure that he or she reads the right words. Use particular responsibilities or job functions to show that your experiences are both significant and have resulted in contributions to your employer.

Maria Lopez was from a family that operated small businesses, including a gravel pit, a lumber yard, a golf course on a resort island, and a new string of condominiums. Maria did not want to note all of her family's holdings on her résumé because she felt it would give the wrong impression. She mentioned that she ran the golf course, was responsible for the maintenance of equipment, and had construction experience with the condos.

She was ready to start interviewing and was hoping to get a good opportunity in industry. Even though she could always go back to the family business, she wanted to make it on her own. She reviewed her résumé with her advisor, and the advisor became spellbound with Maria's experience and accomplishments. Her family had given her significant responsibility, not only in running a business but in building the business. An examination of the résumé clearly indicated that the experience and competence Maria possessed was not evident, so they started to categorize Maria's accomplishments.

Under the categories of project management, business plans, supervision, marketing and promotion, and zoning variances, Maria had significant experience. Her family let her negotiate and manage subcontracts with construction firms, prepare a submittal for zoning variances for the condos, and plan a new use for the gravel pit that would potentially realize significant gain. In each area, not only did she have valuable experience, her contributions to the business were significant. One example was the following.

Business Development: Organized and implemented a plan to expand a golf course to 18 holes and conducted a promotional campaign that tripled membership the first year. This move boosted the adjoining condo business, which had been flat.

Over and over, there were incredible accomplishments that were not evident. Maria had assumed that anyone would have achieved the same success if they had the same opportunities she had, which is not so.

When Maria entered her first interview with a Fortune 100 company, the interviewer rose to greet her and shook her hand. Then she said, "Congratulations. I have reviewed 39 résumés, and yours is the only one I remember. You chose topics I want to see, and you listed what your contribution was. Most people only say what they do. I have been looking forward to meeting you." Maria did well with interviewing, received several competitive offers, and eventually went with an electric utility to assume responsibilities in marketing and project management.

It is clear in this example that the manner of presentation is as important to the recruiter as are the facts. Your presentation and your accomplishments are necessary to establish your credibility with prospective employers. To give further consideration to the perspectives of recruiters and management, consider the following examples. Although numerous, they are concise and reflect an understanding of industry.

Construction Progress Monitoring: Tracked subcontractor's progress to maintain schedule and ensure that specifications were met.

Communications: Prepared and delivered presentations for sales and upper management personnel regarding potential plant modifications. An excellent opportunity to gain first-hand knowledge of management decision processes.

Cost Control: Monitored expenditures and investigated all questionable entries. As a result, overruns were reduced by 10 percent.

Counseling: Worked closely with handicapped students and campers while they spent two weeks in the wilderness. A fascinating opportunity to learn about other perspectives.

Customer Service: Enjoyed the daily interaction with customers and responsibility of understanding and resolving their concerns. Received customer satisfaction recognition award.

Database Design: Developed process to generate quality plans for all electrical switches and maintained complete document control.

Database Management: Created part-recognition codes for an automated part-creation system using VAX, Data General, Honeywell, and IBM mainframes. Code structure was successfully implemented.

Design Support: Developed and supported Lotus command language programs and spreadsheets for design engineering calculations and test data compilation. Offered an excellent opportunity to work with senior design engineers and to witness the design process.

Estimating: Developed project budget with project manager. Assisted in the development of bids. All contracts received were completed on time and within budget.

Finance: Responsible for banking and bookkeeping. Completed a present-value analysis for a major purchase versus repair decision.

Information Management: Participated in the software development and successful implementation of a bar-coded inspection data-management system.

Information Systems: Mastered and utilized in-house software system and PC spreadsheet software to display plant production indicators.

Instruction: Presented classes on equipment maintenance, safety, and first aid.

Instruction: Successfully trained users in operation of IBM mainframe MRP system.

Inventory Management: Monitored inventory performance and reduced "dead" inventory by 70 percent. Developed database to track inventory performance.

Inventory Management: Concurrently reduced total inventory while increasing availability of critical replacement parts for the customer.

Inventory Management: Assisted in the reduction of in-house surplus inventory by more than $1 million.

JIT: Expedited purchase orders as required to accommodate shop needs.

Liaison: Functioned as connection between woods and plastics and engineering, drafting, shipping, receiving, and other in-house manufacturing facilities.

Management: Developed and operated a company that offered lawn care and landscaping services, a lucrative business that grew to 80 clients and 6 employees.

Manufacturing: Established production flow-line balancing in manufacturing area. Successful in working with others, ranging from blue collar to management. Enjoyed the role of facilitator.

Materials Testing: Conducted concrete and soil tests measuring slump, air entrainment, compression, sieve analysis, proctors, and moisture content.

MRP: Provided interface among shop and purchasing functions to assure timely delivery of all raw materials while maintaining material input budget.

Negotiations: Helped reduce procurement costs for office supplies through effective negotiation of supplies contract.

Planning and Scheduling: Developed a computer-driven PERT/CPM model for construction coordination. Program was successfully implemented.

Preconstruction Planning: Worked with a design team to accommodate owner's demands while satisfying architectural requirements.

Procedure Development: Analyzed manufacturing operations and developed procedures for critical assembly operations. Procedures have successfully been placed in service.

Process Development and Implementation: Made significant modifications to the existing quality system, including inspection instructions, calibration specifications and procedures, inspection device numbering system, and quality plans.

Procurement: Analyzed vendors and prepared specifications. Helped to implement new quality-improvement program. Conducted inventory-cost analysis.

Production: Responsible for the setup and operation of production machine tools.

Programming: As part of a multimillion dollar contract, I successfully rewrote software for a twenty-year-old computerized quality system to current Fortran 77 standards.

Project Supervision: Monitored concrete pours to assure specifications were being met, while getting exposure to the various activities and problems associated with the construction industry.

Project Support: Maintained and organized contract documents for numerous construction projects to track progress and scope changes.

Project Troubleshooting: Consulted with the project engineer in resolving drawing discrepancies encountered on the field.

Proposal Development: Participated in efforts to generate marketing proposals. Assisted in corporate proposal to upgrade branch information system.

Quality: Contacted dealerships to pinpoint the warranty problems on all new vehicles.

Quality Control: Received award for production quality performance. Developed procedures to reduce scrap rate. Analyzed defective products and developed a successful strategy for improving product.

Quality Development: Recommended and presented opportunities to improve co-op and intern programs to the executive directors. Recommendations were accepted and implemented.

Quality Improvement: An outstanding opportunity to contribute to quality improvement. Made several recommendations for procedural changes that were successfully implemented.

RFQs: Prepared requests for quotes and expedited the bidding process. Evaluated bids and awarded contracts for various components of the project to subcontractors.

Sales: Regularly exceeded sales quotas and contributed $150,000 sales volume in a highly competitive market. Enjoyed working with customers and understanding their needs.

Sales/Customer Service: Assisted customers with their needs regarding both purchases and applications. Enjoyed resolving problems and contributed to increased sales.

Sales Training: Responsible for training of new employees to meet customer needs and promote business. Developed a successful program for improving customer service and sales.

Scheduling: Developed and maintained a work schedule for several construction projects. Scheduling effort contributed to successful contract completion.

Scheduling: Assisted in just-in-time and pull scheduling; helped maintain a schedule compliance of 95 percent. Average production of engine cooling motors was 6500 per shift.

Supervision: Directed in-house trades and various subcontractors on a seven-story parking garage for the hospital in Norwood.

Supervision: Responsibility for forty union employees required job assignments, discipline, and working with union representatives. Addressed employee grievances in management policy and overtime hours.

Supervision: Managed a production crew of five. This was an excellent opportunity to work with a range of people in meeting production demands. Production rates increased by 8 percent.

Technical Communications: Composed chapter for procedural manual to diagnose equipment malfunctions.

Testing: Developed test procedures for defective parts. Assisted in testing of materials for flaws.

Testing: Responsible for UL testing, inspection, and quarterly audits.

Time Studies: Reduced labor hours and increased shift

production standards, which saved money.

Training: Responsible for the training of several new employees in all areas of the machine line.

Training: Successfully trained several new employees on operations of department.

Training: Trained replacement co-op student in order to make a smooth transition.

Troubleshooting: Conducted analysis and testing of unacceptable products that led to the general improvement of product and/or process performance.

Topics need not be presented in alphabetical order; in fact, it is reasonable that the most important topics be placed first. On rare occasions, the topical areas of expertise may be extended to include specific high-level classroom projects, management responsibilities for student organizations, or possibly volunteer activities, if such information is not included under additional information. Do not include experience that is unrelated or otherwise insignificant.

The preceding list was drawn from the experiences of students to offer the reader a range of ideas for presenting experience. For individuals who are well into their careers, this same format remains highly effective but should be much easier to complete.

Additional Information

Although several headings can be used, it is easier to include all the remaining information under the broad umbrella of Additional Information and use bold subheadings to direct the reader, just as you did with your objective and experience. Information should be included that is important to your prospective employer.

Academic Honors: Presidential Scholar (3 sem.), Dean's List, Electrical Engineering Outstanding Sophomore Award.

Activities: Member, Professional Skaters Guild of America; Member, Interdisciplinary Engineering and Management Society.

Activities: Clarkson Ambassadors' Charter Day and

Founders Day Chairperson, Entrepreneurs Club, Women's Center Co-coordinator, Intramural Sports.

Activities: TDK social fraternity (steward), hunting, fishing, and golf. Avid audiophile and also enjoy early twentieth-century literature. Licensed glider pilot.

Activities: Vice President, Interdisciplinary Engineering and Management Society; Member, Associated General Contractors of America.

Additional Employment: Sales, landscaping, bartender-waitress.

Coaching: Youth hockey, power skating.

College Funding: Have funded 90 percent of college expenses through scholarships, loans, and work.

College Funding: Part-time employment, in conjunction with scholarship support and loans, have enabled me to cover 80 percent of all college-related expenses.

Competition—Motorcycle Racing: Nationally ranked with over 200 trophies won.

Computer-Aided Manufacturing Project: A group project involving designing a program using Mastercam that commands a computer numerical control machine to accomplish a specified task.

Computer Proficiency: CAD/CAM packages, spreadsheets, graphics, and databases.

Computer Proficiency: Literate in IBM and Apple Macintosh. Trained in BASIC, Lotus 1–2–3, Excel, Microsoft Word, WordPerfect, PageMaker, Primavera, MacProject, MacDraft, and Databases.

Computer Skills: Knowledge of spreadsheets, databases, simulation programs, electronic mail, and word processors.

Design Project: Led a team effort to design and build a solar-powered automobile. Successfully competed with thirty other universities in a race from New Orleans to Detroit. Currently forming a design team for a human-powered ICBM.

Forecasting Project: Developed forecasting program for national marketing managers. Predicted probable shifts in share of market for various market segments, allowing appropriate action to be initiated sooner.

Foreign Language: Fluent in French and can understand most Italian. Lived in Europe during my senior year of high school.

Foreign Language—French: J'ai une bonne connaissance du français. Ma mère est francophone, j'ai pris quatre ans de cours et, le cas échéant, je suis disposé à continuer mes études, et il me serait facile d'améliorer mon français.

Honors: Presidential Scholar Spring 1992, Dean's List, Board of Trustees' Scholarship, Freshman Academic Award, St. Peter Marian Golf Scholarship, Fusaro, Altomare & Ermillio Law Firm Scholarship, Assistant Program Chairperson of Sigma Tau Iota —Engineering and Management Honor Society.

Honors: Presidential Scholar, Dean's List (3), Sigma Tau Iota Honor Society.

Honors: Dean's List; The National Dean's List.

Independent Project—Early Career Performance: Developed, conducted, and analyzed a study of 720 graduates on career success.

Information Systems Project: Designed telecommunications system for commercial sales group. This system included an extensive database of various information and modem connections to allow sales force outside access to this information.

Interests: Hockey, golf, tennis.

Leadership/Offices: President, Senior Class; President, ASME; Ice Carnival Cochairman, Assistant House Manager, Alpha Chi Rho National Fraternity.

Civic Affairs: Member of school board, active in Rotary Club.

Leisure Activities: Avid golfer; enjoy tennis, sailing, and other water sports.

Market Analysis Project: Completed analysis of commercial heat pump market. Included were estimates of the availability of technology and various energy sources, possible competitive action, and recommendations for corporate strategies.

Miscellaneous: Financed 40 percent of college education.

Music: Alto saxophone, jazz and classical solo performance.

Music: Guitarist in an R&B band. This was a fun diversion while studying engineering and helped cover educational expenses. First flutist with the Norwood symphony.

Opera: Studied voice and dance for nine years and have performed in several major productions in Cleveland.

Projects—Materials Science: Analyzed compressive strength of concrete cylinders and mortar cubes. **Information Systems:** Created unique database system for a video rental store.

Publications: IEEE student section award-winning paper on the structural mounting requirements for solar cells on an automobile.

Recreation: Intramural athletics, enjoy golf.

Sales Project: Accompanied commercial regional sales manager on field sales trip. This included discussion of possible sales techniques to be used by both the company and its distributors and new-product introduction and discussion with area contractors concerning changes in the market and possible adjustments in response to these changes.

Sports: Captain of NYS championship high school basketball team. Enjoy rugby, golf, and handball.

Sports Officiating: Registered USA hockey official (1982–1992). Received three scholarships to attend Olympic training camps and a National Hockey League clinic.

Student Senator: Budgeting, finance, and constitutions.

System Simulation Project: Developed, executed, and analyzed a manufacturing problem appropriate to discrete simulation using the Siman simulation language and illustrated that model with Cinema, the companion simulation animation language.

Volunteer Work: Diocesan Youth Commission, Province II Youth Network, Parish Vestry Search Committee.

Volunteer Work: Coaching (baseball, hockey), tutoring, fund raising (Christmas toy drive), officiating (basketball).

Volunteer Work: Hockey coach for a team of eight-year-old children, teaching the basic concepts and rules of hockey. This was one of my most rewarding experiences, watching young children develop over the course of a season. Instructed USA Hockey clinics in New York State.

Volunteer Work: Tutor, soccer coach, little league umpire, coat drive, road races for charity.

Travel/Relocation: No restrictions on travel. Southern/western location preferred for living.

References: Available upon request.

As with the section on experience, topics should be ordered by importance to the prospective employer. *Travel*, *Relocation*, and *References* are closure topics to be placed at the end. Before you finalize this section, reflect once more on your interests, accomplishments, and abilities; you may have something important to include under important information on your résumé. One student forgot to mention that he had worked as an interpreter; it was nowhere evident that he was trilingual.

Frank Cortez, a citizen of Costa Rica, was completing his senior year and wanted a job in industry. He had a strong academic record and his involvement with activities outside of the classroom was notable as well. Most of the companies interviewing on campus specified U.S. citizenship, and he was unsuccessful in the interviews he did get. Frank had already decided that he wanted to work toward U.S. green-card status, but that decision naturally had little effect on the recruiters with whom he met.

His level of frustration was mounting, and graduation was two weeks away. Frank knew he would have to return home after graduation if he did not find a good opportunity, and he saw his chances for finding a good position even further reduced. With the little time left, he scheduled a meeting to discuss career-search strategy with his advisor.

Two critical points were identified at their meeting. First, Frank had presented an overly general objective on his résumé. There were particular opportunities he was looking for, but he did not want to rule out others. His principal interests were in project-related tasks such as proposal development, scheduling, and field engineering. These interests were not evident on his résumé and were not discussed at several of the interviews he did have. Frank prepared a more specific objective that addressed why these areas were of interest to him.

The second point was a significant error of omission; Frank neglected to mention that he was trilingual and had worked as an interpreter for a trade company, translating proposals and bids from two dialects of Chinese to English and Spanish! This fact was incorporated into his résumé, and it allowed him to mention the extended periods that he had lived in Asia.

Within three weeks Frank was interviewed for, and subsequently offered, a position as project manager for servicing the manufacturing industry. Frank contacted me six months after he commenced work to let me know that he was doing well and was happy. He was concluding a project in Venezuela and bidding on a job in the Philippines. It is true that he had unusual qualifications. But he also had unusual hurdles, which had made employment prospects seem bleak until he saw how to relate his strengths with the needs of a prospective employer.

Your résumé is a document of fact. Any subjective information will weaken the strength of the facts you have included. For example, your writing demonstrates your communications skills, so you don't need to state that you have developed good ones. Stick to facts, and the reviewer will see that you are direct in communication and will accept your information as factual.

People seldom include first-person perspectives in their résumé, yet this may be the most direct path for establishing a relationship of candor with a prospective employer. If you decide to include personal perspectives, they should reflect your positive side. They ought to show enthusiasm, or deliberate thought processes, or in some cases, you can express gratitude for prior responsibilities you have held.

In your objective you can include a sentence that better describes the environment or responsibilities you want. If you are honest with yourself when you write this, your prospective employer will come to know you more quickly, and you may even open other alternatives. You may have expressed a desire to work in production because you liked the challenge of working with others under the pressure of time. The recruiter may not have a production job, but he or she may have another position that exactly meets your criteria. Some examples for consideration are these:

I enjoy competition and working under the stress of time pressure.

The ideal organization will be committed to excellence and, therefore, committed to and demanding of employee development.

My preference is for hands-on responsibilities. The ideal position will require knowledge of manufacturing equipment and a rapport with its operators.

Under *Experience* or *Activities*, you can use such comments to help draw the recruiter's interest and questions. They seem to work most effectively when they are presented as a closing thought or observation for a given employer or activity. Again, these ought to be heartfelt and not just a set of words that you have conjured up. You may well have experiences that are important to you— don't be afraid to say so.

I am grateful for the opportunity to work among the functional areas of design, testing, and customer service.

The discipline required to become a recognized ballerina has helped me to effectively face career-related challenges as well.

I was fortunate to have a demanding boss who was dedicated to the strategic development of the individuals in her organization.

Candid observations like the preceding ones can help you to project a positive attitude and invite conversation. They are useful for offering relevant perspectives that might otherwise be overlooked by the recruiter. If you elect to include personal perspectives, no more than two or three comments should be included, and you should be prepared to discuss them honestly and enthusiastically.

I have placed so much emphasis on the résumé because once you have done a credible job in completing it, you will likely have developed a clearer perception of what your significant accomplishments and goals are. This kind of focus is even more important for growth within an organization.

Unless you have a significant range and depth of experience, your résumé should be limited to one page. In addition, the layout should offer a lot of white space, which helps to keep the important points you want to make from being buried. Cole (1985) lists mistakes of form (longer than two pages, cute, including photographs, etc), and mistakes of substance (falsification, rambling, etc.). Two examples are shown, each projecting the individual's interests and accomplishments being somewhat in line with the objective. In each case, the individual does not yet have post-college experience. One case projects resonance for an individual with a nontechnical background and objective.

After the Résumé

The topics of networking, the search, the interview, and letter writing are covered well in other resources. Selected comments appear here, and the reader is advised to review the annotated listing of relevant publications in Appendix B for source material.

Comments Regarding Business Letters

Cover letters submitted with a résumé are often not read. When résumés are circulated within an organization, they are often sent without the cover letter. However, a good business letter can have a profound affect. A young woman was seeking a position with an architect-engineering firm. The firm was scheduled to visit campus but was not scheduled to interview candidates from her major. She sent a short but well-written letter to a director in this company detailing her career objectives and explaining her academic major. He was so impressed with her ability to write a good letter that he showed it to his supervisors, remarking that few in the department could write that well. His instruction to the recruiter scheduled to visit the campus was, "I don't care who you interview up there as long as you meet with this individual." She got the interview, and she subsequently received an offer.

Probably the most common faults found in letters are spelling and grammatical errors, awkward choice of words, and excessive use of I as a word. Other typical problems are excessive length, the use of casual language, the point of the letter being buried, and poor organization. Learn how to get to the point in the opening sentence of all business communications, including

Jamar Warner
1500 Willow Street
Ludwig, OH 12345
(999) 555-1234

OBJECTIVE

Project Management/Proposal Development: Seek responsibilities in project coordination, equipment testing and turnover, and extensive customer interface. The ideal firm is a recognized competitor in its market, is demanding of its employees, and rewards good performance.

EDUCATION

MID-EASTERN UNIVERSITY, Ludwig, OH
Interdisciplinary Engineering & Management, B.S., May 1994, GPA 3.18/4.0

EXPERIENCE

SMYTH-DOE, Ludwig, OH (Fall 92 - Summer 93)
Co-op: Applications Engineering - Marketing
Continuous Improvement - Worked with engineers, product specialists, and cost department to improve efficiency and accuracy of proposal and price-estimation process.
Proposal Preparation - Assisted in $15 million proposal of three reciprocating compressors by using company engineering programs to determine primary machine components needed to meet customer requirements.

Co-op: Industrial Engineering
Project Management - Evaluated and implemented several capital expenditure projects focused on improving quality, productivity, and safety.
Environmental Engineering - Participated in environmental projects including plant inspections, meeting government regulations, and reducing hazardous waste.
ISO 9000 - Used CAD to create drawings for assembly tools and revised a training matrix to document qualifications of manufacturing engineering group in preparation for ISO audit.
Plant Renovations - Directed plant renovations including office expansions and construction of tool crib to control availability of tools.
OSHA - Addressed several areas of concern for meeting safety requirements to prepare for OSHA inspection.

MONTGOMERY FEND, Ludwig, OH (5/89 - 8/91)
Lawn and Garden Equipment
Commission Sales - Leading sales performance for entire period of time.

ADDITIONAL INFORMATION

College Funding - Contributed over $60,000 toward college expenses through scholarships, grants, job earnings, and loans.
Computer Skills - CAD, databases, spreadsheets, desktop publishing, word processors.
Academic Honors - Dean's List: Spring 91, Fall 92, Spring 93.
Men's Basketball - JV Captain 1991-92.

REFERENCES

Available upon request.

ALANA WASHINGTON

1500 Willow Street
Ludwig, OH 12345
(999) 555-1234

OBJECTIVE
Manufacturing: A position combining technical and analytical competence with an opportunity to become an effective leader. The ideal organization is committed to total quality and stresses communication, leadership, and self-motivation.

EDUCATION
MID-EASTERN UNIVERSITY, Ludwig, OH
Bachelor of Science, **Mechanical Engineering,** May 1993, GPA 3.82

NEBRASKA MARITIME ACADEMY, Omaha, NE
Majored in Marine Transportation, 8/89 – 12/89, GPA 3.67

EXPERIENCE
MAJOR ELECTRIC, Ludwig, OH (1/92 – 8/92)
Steam Turbine Engineering Systems Co-op
Programming: As part of a multi-million dollar contract, I rewrote software for a 20-year-old computerized quality system to current Fortran 77 standards.
Database Management: Created part recognition codes for an automated part creation system using VAX, Data General, Honeywell, and IBM mainframes.
Design Support: Developed and supported Lotus command language programs and spreadsheets for design engineering calculations.
Quality Improvement: Recommended and presented opportunities to improve co-op and intern programs to the executive directors.

MID-EASTERN UNIVERSITY, Ludwig, OH (1/91 – 8/91, 9/92 – 5/93)
Tutor/Peer Mentor
Tutor: Tutored Calculus II, Physics I, and Accounting I.
Peer Mentor: Successfully helped students on academic probation return to good standing through peer mentoring and tutoring.

SKI AND SAIL, Ludwig, OH (1/87 – 1/91)
Certified Ski Technician and Sailboard Instructor/Rental Coordinator
Quality Assurance and Maintenance: Certified by six major ski-binding manufacturers to perform ski mounting and maintenance functions. Routinely performed binding release checks to ensure manufacturer accuracy and customer safety.
Instruction: Conducted sailboard lessons for individuals from 13 to 70 years old.
Customer Service: Rented sailboards and paddleboats for off-season revenue production.

REFERENCES
Available upon request.

Eric Olsen
1500 Willow Street
Ludwig, OH 12345
(999) 555-1234

OBJECTIVE

Quality Improvement in Manufacturing: Enjoy the challenging responsibilities of Quality Control and can make a measurable contribution to business. My experience has confirmed my desire to improve quality at a manufacturing company.

EDUCATION

MID-EASTERN UNIVERSITY, Ludwig, OH
Bachelor of Science, **Electrical Engineering**

EXPERIENCE

MARQUARDT SWITCHES, INC., Cazenovia, NY
ISO 9000 - Participated in quality planning.
Process Development and Implementation - Made significant modifications to the existing quality system, including inspection instructions, calibration specifications and procedures, inspection device numbering system, and quality plans.
Testing - Responsible for UL testing, inspection, and quarterly audits.
Database Design - Developed system to determine quality plans for all switches and maintained complete document control.
Troubleshooting - Conducted analysis and testing of unacceptable products which led to the general improvement of product and/or process performance.
Information Management - Participated in the software development and successful implementation of a bar coded inspection data management system

CONSOLIDATION ELECTRIC, Ludwig, OH
MRP - Interfaced between shop and purchasing to assure timely delivery of all raw materials while maintaining material input budget.
Inventory Management - Assisted in reducing in-house surplus inventory.
JIT - Expedited purchase orders as required and canceled or delayed orders to meet the shop's needs.
Liaison - Functioned as connection between Woods and Plastics and Engineering, Drafting, Shipping, Receiving, and other in-house manufacturing facilities.

ADDITIONAL INFORMATION

LEADERSHIP:
College Union Board - Entertainment contract negotiations, programming and booking, National Convention delegate, program development
Student Senate - Budgeting, finance, and constitutions.

Computer Proficiency - SPC software, spreadsheets, databases, word processing, mainframes, programming, graphics, communications.
Volunteer Work - Diocesan Youth Commission, Province II Youth Network, Parish Vestry Search Committee.
Other Interests - Guitar, tennis, golf, travel.

REFERENCES

Available upon request.

ROSE STEINFELD

1500 Willow Street
Ludwig, OH 12345
(999) 555-1234

OBJECTIVE
Manufacturing - Process efficiency is a principle interest of mine. Experiences with JIT, MRP, and the empowering of hourly workers demonstrate that these concepts can help any company increase its efficiency. The ideal opportunity will include a manufacturing training program, which would further develop my skills to make me a better employee.

EDUCATION
MID-EASTERN UNIVERSITY, Ludwig, OH
Bachelor of Science, **Mechanical Engineering,** May 1994, **GPA 3.92/4.0**

EXPERIENCE
GENERAL CORPORATION, Ludwig, OH (1/93 – 8/93)
Manufacturing/Quality Engineer, Co-Op
Vendor Coordination: Consulted with vendors to design and install two dust collection systems and a bulk caulking system. Systems installed on-time and were operational upon my departure.
— Interacted with several OEM's in capability study of various manufacturers' rivet guns and feasibility of installation on the assembly line.
Labor Relations: Collaborated with union labor teams, production supervisors, and vendors to design and implement safety and ergonomic improvements to assembly line operations.
ISO 9000: Monitored cleanliness of container unit component parts and created specifications to facilitate continued ISO certification.
Production Support: Proactively supported production during introduction of R-134a refrigeration units.
JIT: Instituted process improvements to a demand flow manufacturing assembly line.
– Participated in groups dedicated to continuous improvement.
Quality Assurance: Developed criteria for and implemented a daily quality audit procedure.

WEGMANS FOOD MARKETS, Ludwig, OH (7/89 - Present)
Operations Management: Directed front-end operations; management of employee operating schedule, delegation of front-end responsibilities, and handling of customer requests.
Customer Service: Processed customer orders in a friendly/expedient manner.
Recognition: Awarded Wegmans Scholarship for academic and work performance excellence.

ADDITIONAL
INFORMATION
College Funding - Personally funded over $40,000 through scholarships, work, and loans.
Computer Experience - Word processors, spreadsheets, databases, and graphics.
Honors/Activities - Inducted into four honorary societies; received numerous awards and scholarships; member of various engineering organizations.
References - Available upon request.

your cover letter. An excellent text by Murphy and Hildebrandt (1988) provides a comprehensive resource for developing letter- and report-writing skills. Meyer and meyer (1986) is also excellent, but less comprehensive and perhaps more to the point.

Locating Opportunities

If you already have a position and are seeking change, you may be overlooking your best opportunities. It is not uncommon for an employee to conduct a search and not recognize the growth potential with his or her current employer until resigning. By that time, it is usually too late to take advantage of the growth potential.

There is no magic formula for finding career opportunities with a new employer. Not all jobs are posted publicly; in fact, some openings are never listed before they are filled, particularly when the company decides to create a position for an individual.

Identifying openings depends upon your goals. If your goal is to locate in Tucson, Arizona, you will draw upon different resources than if your goal is to do design and analysis in the aerospace industry. Following are some suggestions.

Trade Magazines. Trade magazines are usually industry specific, and they can be a good source of information. Once a job is listed in a trade magazine, however, it may be too late. They are sometimes slow in listing and can draw a hoard of applications. What you can learn is which companies have new work or are expanding. If these companies are of interest to you, do not wait for a job posting; it may be too late by then. Articles are sometimes written by individuals well placed in an organization. If an article is of interest, contact the author. You may get some excellent leads, along with a chance to avoid the customary screening by the human resources office.

Newspapers. City papers are useful for finding opportunities in that city as well as others. Companies that recruit engineers frequently place ads in regions in which their competitors are located. In this way, a paper such as the *Boston Globe* can be a good resource for jobs in electronics, defense, field engineering, and project management opportunities all over the world. The

Sunday papers seem to be the best, and you might use your library to look at papers from Atlanta, Boston, Chicago, Dallas, Los Angeles, New York, Raleigh, St. Louis, San Francisco, Seattle, or Washington, D.C.

As with the trade journals, consider all companies that reflect business activity. If they are recruiting for a number of engineering management positions, they will probably be looking for field engineers or design engineers as well, even though those positions are not listed, to your knowledge.

By the time a position is posted in the paper, it may be too late. The *Wall Street Journal, Business Week,* and the business sections of regional papers will have articles about companies that are growing or that have recently been awarded major contracts. These articles offer the job hunter more valuable and timely information than the want ads do. Perhaps you can fill a position before the employer goes through the time and expense of advertising that position.

Telephone. If you know what you want (if you don't, go back to the beginning of this chapter), you should be aware of a number of firms that relate to your interests. Call them. With the telephone, you can get the name and address of the vice president of engineering, the plant manager(s), or others who hold key positions that relate to your interests. You can also request product literature, an annual report, and promotional information the company may use in recruiting talent. Usually the receptionist can get you this information. Be courteous and to the point. Even if you mishandle a telephone call, it isn't likely that management will hear about you. They have other things to keep them occupied.

Eight excellent, common-sense tips are offered for telephone etiquette in the IEEE—USA's *Employment Guide*, edited by Backe (1991). The italicized comments are mine.

1. Ask whether this is a convenient time to talk. *You will only alienate the individual if you inconvenience them, and your respect for their schedule demands will be appreciated. Their convenience and your success are directly related!*

2. Begin your conversations by renewing your relationship

with the contact. *He or she likely interfaces with many others and may have difficulty placing you or understanding why you wish to speak with him or her. Help the person remember who you are.*

3. When contacting people in your secondary network, begin your conversations by referring to the person who put you in touch with each person. *Help the person understand why it reasonable that the two of you should share a conversation, and avoid placing him or her at a disadvantage or in an uncomfortable position.*

4. Be direct about the reason for the call. *Your contact needs to know the purpose of the conversation immediately, and he or she recognizes that you have full respect for that person's time.*

5. Let the contact know that you would like to send your résumé and a list of the companies in which you are interested. *Although I do not feel as strongly about this point, the purpose is to condition the individual to expect to receive—and thus respond to—your résumé. If the contact is aware of openings elsewhere, it is hoped that he or she will share this information with you. Like most of the other points, this tactic is taken directly from selling strategy.*

6. Establish a time at which you can call back. *This is another nudge intended to gain the individual's commitment to addressing your interest in their organization.*

7. Follow up your conversation the same day with a letter of thanks. *You want to take every opportunity to help the individual to remember you. You also want him or her to recognize that you can write well and that you follow through quickly. If commitments are made to provide information, schedule another call, or have you visit the company offices or if the person expressed enthusiasm for your qualifications, use your letter to document his or her commitments and enthusiasm. Your letter should be brief, thus allowing these points to stand out.*

8. Call back on schedule. *You want to show that you are deliberate in your communications and scheduling. Also,*

don't let the person off the hook. If he or she is not pre-pared to talk with you, be prepared to ask them for a defi-nition of the ideal candidate for the position, and sched-ule another telephone call. You ought to learn something helpful from the answer to your question and obtain a commitment for the rescheduled call.

Headhunters. Headhunters are a pain in the neck, but they know about opportunities of which you may be unaware. Also, you may be able to learn something from them. Some are good at coaching a candidate for an interview and will help the applicant compensate for deficiencies and overcome faults. All charge money, but usually the company picks up the fee. I am personally against paying a headhunter.

Think for a minute about how headhunters make money. Usually they are paid by the firm for each position that they are able to help the company fill. It may be a percentage of the start-ing salary, or it may be a fixed fee. So what do the headhunters want most? They want to fill positions. First, they want the company to like you well enough to extend you an offer. Once this is accomplished, they want you to say yes, and they know how to put pressure on you to accept an offer. The company, on the other hand, wants to hire people who really want to work for them. Clients who say "Thanks, but no thanks" do not earn any money for a headhunter.

Working with headhunters is more likely as you enter the ranks of management. Whatever your station, be ready to hold out for what you want. If you don't have the reins on them, they may instead have the reins on you. Unless you find good head-hunters and are able to exercise some control over a project, you may find the situation becoming quite stressful. You should ex-pect to work closely and candidly with them, and you may find that you learn a lot from headhunters as well.

Kenneth Cole (1985) suggests an interesting system for clas-sifying people as either A's or B's (41). In his model, members of the A group are not seeking a job change, and the members of the B group are. He makes the point that members of the B group are perceived to have more problems, such as termination, per-sonality conflict, and the like. Accordingly, your reasons of availability and interest regarding a job opening must be substantial in a manner that helps prospective employers dispel such concerns.

Associates/Clients/Friends. Learn about what is going on in your industry from those with whom you work. Family friends may be well placed and can help you out. They may be able to identify upcoming needs, or they may be able to tell you not to waste your time because of the poor business conditions. Communicate with others and keep abreast of what is happening beyond your own immediate environment.

Professional Societies. Professional societies are an excellent idea. Participants tend to be proactive individuals and offer the dual advantage of informing you of opportunities and becoming your advocate from within the organization. IEEE is one of the most effective engineering organizations, particularly when you start reaching into the realm of engineering management. Others include ASME, ANS, ASEE (particularly if you wish to teach engineering), and AMA, to mention a few. I am also an advocate for community involvement. Junior Achievement is a nationwide organization that helps high school students organize small business venture groups. Typically, Junior Achievement is actively supported by industry leaders from the area.

Regional Aids. In addition to the local chapters of professional organizations, ask your local chamber of commerce for information regarding area businesses. Office-supply firms and banks usually know the companies that are growing. Talk to them.

The Company, the Boss, the Location

A 1992 survey of recent graduates (see Appendix A) from Clarkson University's Engineering and Management Program offers perspective on how new hires perceive their workplace and career progress. Certainly, it is worth knowing what your criteria are for defining a good employer, boss, and location before you commence your search; yet these remain pervasive questions once you have an offer in hand.

A relocation is sometimes difficult to contemplate. Only fifty percent of the graduates surveyed wanted to relocate, yet 80 percent did. Ninety-six percent of those who have relocated said it was a beneficial experience. When asked if a move was personally beneficial, recent graduates offered the following comments:

> *Extremely! I highly recommend experiencing new locations. People's attitudes and values vary greatly from coast to coast. Helps to redefine your ideals.*

> *I relocated one year into my career and found it tremendously rewarding. I made new friends, met different customers, learned a new city, and experienced different cultures. I gained a great deal of flexibility.*

> *Absolutely. Moving forces independence. Your ability to adapt to new people and surroundings is a good measure of your self-confidence, which, in turn, affects career performance. Each job teaches you new skills, and each mentor adds to the collection of styles you can use to form your own style.*

> *No. You lose a lot of support systems and have to build them all over again.*

> *One of the most important things one can learn is how to develop friends from strangers. It is very beneficial to learn how to appear (to be) comfortable in uncomfortable situations or environments.*

With so much emphasis on getting a job offer, it is difficult to focus on the characteristics of a "good" organization or manager (see Appendix A for further information). For the work environment, the characteristics most often cited as important include advancement potential, financial stability (of the organization), benefits and pay, and active support of employee development and growth.

It is sometimes said that the company for which you work is as good as the person for whom you work; this phrase has merit. Recent graduates clearly want most a boss who listens well. Other frequently cited criteria include effective leadership, communication skills, understanding and support, and fairness.

The Interview

The opportunity to interview is a result of a successful career-search effort. The interview is a critical time, where both parties have mutual interest in knowing one another better. It is easy to get nervous about an interview, and many enter an interview with a pessimistic attitude about their candidacy. This, of course, works against you, so it may be worthwhile to look at this event in the following way. Regardless of how the interview is approached, the interviewer most likely hopes that you will be the number one candidate for the position. They hope this because they want to meet their objectives for the day, just as you want to meet yours. Also, people who interview candidates usually have other responsibilities as well. The sooner that they can conclude the search, the sooner they can get back to their primary responsibilities. In fact, most recruiters consider interviewing important, but often tedious.

In making preparations, remember that an interview is really a two-way street. You want to learn more about the company and the available position to see if this is the job most suitable to you and your capabilities. The goal of the interviewer is to find the best person available for the job as soon as possible and in the best possible way. Take a look at yourself from the interviewer's point of view. Are you the person for whom the interviewer is looking? You can be, with some preparation. Adequate preparation includes the following:

- *Know yourself.* This is the most important preparation. It should have already been done when putting together your résumé. You should know the job or job area you want, the requirements for the job, and how your qualifications compare with the requirements. Presumably, this has been accomplished before your résumé is finalized.

- *Research the company.* Get some facts about the company. Reference materials are available from the company, the library, the college placement office, and from professional/business journals. You should know a brief history of the company, plant and office locations, types of products or services, its growth over the years, and its prospects for the future.

- *Research the market.* Knowledge about competition, technology, market dynamics, and regulatory issues will help you keep the interview on the "big picture."

- *Present yourself well.* Because the very first impression you make will carry through the entire interview and will help to determine its outcome, it is important to project a positive image. The clothes you wear and your overall neatness affect your impact on the interviewer.
- *Check details about the interview.* Know when and where the interview will be held and be there early. You should know the full name and address of the company, the interviewer's name and title, and how to pronounce his or her name. You may also want to bring a notebook or folder and pen.

Donald Asher identifies several rules to follow in the interview (1993):

1. Make eye contact, but don't stare down your interviewer.
2. Never contradict, interrupt, or argue with your interviewer.
3. Be alert, act interested, and focus on the positive.
4. Never, never, never say anything bad about your former employers.

What Do Interviewers Look For?

The most important aspect that many interviewers look for is focus. It reflects self-confidence; you know what you like and want to do. Self-confident individuals communicate more clearly and are more believable.

They also look at your interests—what you want to do and why you want to do it, your goals, interest in continuing education, geographic preference, and willingness to relocate. Your interests ought to relate well to your objective and to the employer's needs. Your facial expressions and body language confirm where your interests really lie.

They consider your personality. First impressions are important. They tell a lot about your poise, ability to communicate, and general social skills.

They look at your qualifications. Grade-point average, work experience, and extracurricular activities are all important. But most important is how all these things relate to your career objectives.

They check to see if you have done your homework. Learn about the company through recruiting literature, annual reports, and the college placement office library. Find out about products, service, sales, earnings, business strategies, benefit programs, and the corporate culture.

They look at your communication. A lot of facts are given in a short time. The interviewer needs enough information to make a decision as to whether the company should invite you for further interviews.

A recruiter's initial evaluation form includes many criteria:

Personal appearance

Manner and attitude

Conversational ability

Background (both educational and experience)

Maturity level

Sense of responsibility

Interview preparation

Drive and initiative

Suggestions for Ending the Interview

Do reiterate your interest in the position and that you are looking forward to a favorable response. Also, leave the interview in the same polite and assured manner you entered. Look the interviewer in the eye, smile, give a firm handshake, and tell him or her that you enjoyed the interview.

Ask for the job!

Who Is Most Likely to Get Hired?

An expressed desire to work and make a contribution is important, demonstrated communication skills are a must, and academic performance is looked at carefully. Good work experience can be very helpful, but the lack of experience can be overcome with strength in the aforementioned qualities. One line manager who participates in college recruiting summarized, "We look for positive, dynamic individuals who are willing to learn, work without direct supervision, and interface with others without conflict."

The toughest challenge in interviews is for candidates to open up and express themselves. Make it your objective to get to know the interviewer and make him or her get to know you. Your candor is the most effective way for you to establish yourself as being legitimately interested. Don't be afraid to state that you want the job. Be ready to close the deal by knowing what offer will be acceptable. An interviewer may be considering several candidates; for him or her to extend an offer usually means a wait of up to two weeks for a decision. If you let the interviewer know that you are ready to make a decision today, you may save a lot of time.

When You Get Rejected. You and the company you interviewed with have invested time in the interview. Regardless of whether or not you think the decision can be reversed, find out from the interviewer what he or she wanted that he or she did not see in you. Try to determine how you can increase your interviewing effectiveness. The interviewer may also be aware of employment opportunities in other organizations. If you want that opportunity above all others, tell the interviewer so and ask what you might do to eventually meet the company's criteria.

TERRIBLE, HE PULLED A TRICK QUESTION; WHY DO YOU WANT TO WORK?

When You Get an Offer. Getting offers is not always easy. You may not be sure that you want the job, or perhaps you are hoping to hear a response from another possibility that interests you more. Maybe the offer isn't high enough. If you have a family, there is more than just yourself to consider. Even when everything is ideal about the job, you may have to relocate and find your way around a new city. It all adds up to a lot of stress.

Throughout your career you will make a lot of decisions, and some of them will be tough. Once a decision is made and you have made a commitment, do not reconsider; turn your efforts toward making your choice a success. It has been said that the only wrong decision is the one you fail to act on and see through to completion.

Chapter 4

You and Your New Job—
Making the Most of Both

Experience is not what happens to a
man; it is what a man does with what
happens to him.

Aldous Huxley

Starting a new job is demanding and stressful. The first job after college also includes the indoctrination to industry. It is your first week at work, and you are meeting other employees and learning their titles and responsibilities, there is a stack of reading material growing on your desk, you have found the bathroom and the vending machines and have made your way through the cafeteria, and yet all this only scratches the surface. Many of your initial observations will be incomplete or otherwise in error. Even if it is your third or fourth job, gaining familiarity, effectiveness, and sense of ease in a new organization is challenging and time consuming.

It was heaven when José finally started work. It had been a difficult task of interviewing on campus and finally receiving an attractive job offer. He was excited to now be a part of an organization that actually designs and builds things. It was also a strange time for him in meeting so many new people, finding a place to live, and learning about the corporate culture—a lot of anxiety. When he started college, José was flanked by hundreds of first-year students who were also adapting to a new environment. Now most of the individuals in the organization seemed established in their careers and personal lives. Apartment hunting, getting a driver's license in another state, learning how to use public transportation for commuting—while not knowing anyone—were a time-consuming challenge. Every day he faced new tasks that had to be completed. They seemed to stretch out in front of him forever; yet each week new tasks were brought to completion. After a few weeks, his task list was shorter and less urgent, but he was spending a lot of money on clothes, rent, utilities, furniture, dishes, and, it seemed, a host of other necessities. After a few weeks José found he had some time to think, to relax, and even to pursue personal interests—once he decided what they should be. In college, he had lived at the fraternity house and played football on the house team. Once he got through the process of acclimation, he would have his evenings and weekends largely to himself.

The department he joined seemed quite friendly, each individual taking time to visit with him and answer any questions he had. Steve was one of the first persons, other than his boss, José met at work. He was helpful in teaching José the ropes and went into some detail in explaining to José how the company really worked—who made the decisions, what was most important, who to watch out for, and shortcuts for getting some of the mundane tasks out of the way. José liked Susan, his manager, but did not see her often or meet with her for any periods of time because of her schedule. She had been forthright with José during the interview, and that was one of the things that made this opportunity so attractive. Susan had been to the point in painting a clear picture of the career opportunities, and that was reassuring to José. He could see where he was going.

As the weeks wore on, José came to feel more comfortable about work. He knew how to get through the day and had completed several minor projects as well. There were boring moments as well—he was required to study the company's policy manual (which nobody seemed to use) and a fair amount of product literature. It was quite interesting at first, but it definitely had its tedious side. José took it in stride as he recognized that learning the manuals was necessary. He was anxious to sink his teeth into a bigger project and apply some of the knowledge he gained at school. So far, it seemed that he really had not used his education. They were not pushing him hard, and some of his days had slack time. Certainly, he could only stare at company manuals for so long.

Most people experience a similar period of getting settled, and José is no exception. He has been able to get to know the people and the routine, has made a few friends, and is able to keep up with the projects given to him. This may become a point of vulnerability for José because he is becoming comfortable. It

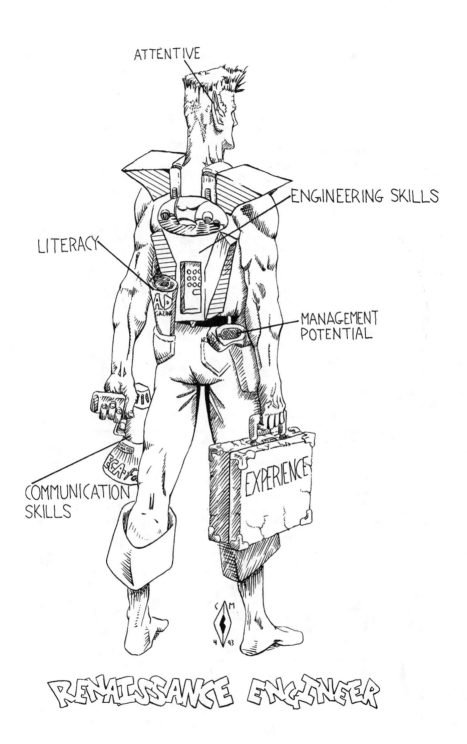

ATTENTIVE

ENGINEERING SKILLS

LITERACY

MANAGEMENT
POTENTIAL

EXPERIENCE

COMMUNICATION
SKILLS

RENAISSANCE ENGINEER

required a focused effort to get the job, and he has concentrated fairly hard in getting adjusted. It may be awhile before José gets any direct feedback regarding his progress.

WHAT NEW HIRES SEE

WHAT MANAGEMENT SEES

After ten months with the firm, José is handling the responsibilities without a problem. We are now to the point where we saw José in the first chapter. He has picked up his work load, and seems to get along well with the department, but the date for his six-month review passed without the promised meeting, expected raise, or even an explanation.

Steve continues to share his views on management with José. Steve believes the company is just using the employees, and with business being down, it is obvious that they have not implemented an effective strategy. According to Steve, José should watch out for himself and think about looking elsewhere to find a real career opportunity. These comments have an effect, and José is starting to echo some of these negative sentiments. He is finding it more difficult to trust his management, so he has become reluctant to discuss his concerns with them. He is now considering a change of jobs and has started updating his résumé. Unfortunately, José is now focused more on the job he wants to escape and is giving too little consideration to what his career goals really are. At this point, any job will be an improvement in José's mind.

Within the past several weeks, José's attitude has become apparent to his supervisor, who, in turn, has expressed concern to Susan. Susan is disappointed that José does not seem to be working out and comments to her director that she may need to recruit a replacement. José has done a pretty good job, but he may be looking to move. Her boss has some disappointing news. If she cannot get José's attitude turned around, he may be part of a necessary reduction. If he leaves, Susan will not be able to replace him. Aaron Bloom suggests that she spend some time with José and find out what his concerns really are. Susan ought to try her level best to maintain her current staffing level.

Susan has grown quickly in the organization, and she considers herself to have strong management potential. However, she would rather spend her time on the business at hand—that is, meeting the design commitments and obtaining additional contracts. Why do people have to get in the way of business progress? Susan is not used to this kind of challenge.

Susan has a good engineering education, she has proven herself to be a capable organizer, and she has effectively completed several important projects—first as a design engineer and later as a supervisor. Good performance and a few timely openings soon resulted in Susan's being promoted to manager. Susan's company had experienced a period of rapid growth that imposed

formidable challenges related to design, manufacturing, material scheduling, and client relations. Her employer attended to
these more pressing needs, while paying insufficient attention to
the development of its management talent. This often happens
when an organization is in a growth mode; unfortunately, it also
happens when the economy is slow. Initially, the organization is
too busy with its own growth to implement or monitor the effectiveness of such programs. Later, when money is tight, management development is an easy target for budget cuts.

We will come back to Susan later, but in light of the potential problems a new employee can encounter, we turn our attention toward positive actions that can be taken by the new employee.

First Things First

With the programs that often exist at work to foster the acclimation and development of new hires, it is easy to forget that the
ultimate responsibility for professional development rests with
the individual alone. Individual responsibility for career performance is often clouded for two reasons. The first is that employers, by offering developmental programs, may appear to have
assumed responsibility for career growth. Secondly, recent graduates have spent most of their life in school, where an obvious
objective is the development and progression of individual students—they expect the organization's mission to be dedicated to
their continued growth! You need only to think of being let go
from a position to realize your own responsibility for the wellbeing of your career. Once you have assumed this responsibility,
constructive measures that you can accomplish seem to follow
naturally.

There are a number of areas, activities, and processes in
each organization that are unfamiliar to the new hire, and it is to
everyone's benefit in the organization to foster an appreciation
and working knowledge of these areas as quickly as possible.
From the management perspective, the employee increases in
efficiency, effectiveness, and breadth of contribution. The recruit's
increased knowledge is a critical step in developing enthusiasm
for addressing the tasks at hand. Several areas of effort are listed

here for your consideration. While reading this you might consider for yourself the value of these recommendations and the extent to which your organization currently emphasizes such development.

Management and Organization Structure

It is well worth understanding the structures of the organization, which should not be taken for granted. Of course, the organization chart and the chain of command above you is a natural starting point, and several copies have perhaps already been provided to you. Organization charts become dated quickly, but more important, they offer little insight as to how groups interface and how responsibilities are delegated. You will likely know what the organization structure is long before you understand how it works.

Next, consider the product(s) produced by each division and how the customer base may vary from product to product and division to division. Is there a reason the structure has the form it does? A functional view of the organization will help you identify the areas containing engineering activities and identify the primary areas of interface for the engineers. For example, does each division do its own engineering, or are there engineering and/or testing activities shared across divisions?

You might then look at how factors such as quality, expenditures, and revenues are managed and how they might impact the engineering and manufacturing functions. Are sales and marketing together (why or why not?), and how might they initiate the new products and product design changes that creates demand for engineering? On the other hand, who might propose changes to the process that will improve reliability, efficiency, flexibility, or quality? How is the money controlled that will be needed to fund product development or process change?

What departments are involved in the life of a purchase order from the time a requisition is made until the goods are received, inspected, and paid for? Commencing with your direct supervisor, learn about the functional responsibilities of each position and each adjacent area. Once completed, proceed upward and outward to learn more about the organization.

It requires talking to people to gain an accurate understanding, because organization charts do not contain the functional information and are often incomplete, out of date, or otherwise in error.

In the context of the organization structure, it is worth getting to know the responsibilities held by your management, starting with your supervisor and proceeding upward and outward. For example, consider the following questions:

- Are all the tasks accomplished by your director's supervisors delegated functionally or by availability of labor?
- What activities and responsibilities consume their time?
- What skills do they consider most important in their own positions, and what do they look for in those working for them?

Individuals With Whom You Work

The more seasoned employees may offer the only historical perspective on the department. Also, they are more likely to have extensive backgrounds beyond the activities of your immediate group. Thus, senior employees can provide you with a first glimpse of areas outside of your current reach. In fact, they may be best able to acquaint you with challenges and growth opportunities that you find exciting.

Other recent hires with whom you work are also learning the ropes. You ought to draw upon each other to better share experiences and avoid wasted effort. You can help identify resources such as individuals, training classes, or company literature that is most helpful for the recent hire.

History

Employee turnover, market changes, reorganization, and product evolution away from traditional lines (and customers) can cause a company to lose a sense of heritage and a sense of mission. One way to make up for your lack of time with your employer is to seek as much historical perspective as is possible. It may be that this information is out of date for the issues currently being faced, but as you come to interface more and more with upper management, your respect for and understanding of company history will be appreciated by others and should reflect maturity on your part. It may be that you need look no further in the past than twenty or thirty years, which is fortunate. There may not be much written literature in your company to help you, so you must depend upon the recollections of those who were employed then. For key events, you may wish to look up articles written in business journals at the time.

Finance

The majority of an organization's decisions are financially driven; to understand its operation, you must understand the flow of money—profits derived from sales, operating expenses, margin, net income, depreciation, and stockholder dividends. Start with a look at how money comes into an organization. Study the sales patterns to understand how the business has grown or changed. A next logical step might be to look into the costs associated with producing and promoting a product. Coincidentally, you ought to gain an understanding of the money, time, and steps required to turn a good idea into a profitable product. It may appear to be trivial, but do you know how $100 of wasted office supplies, wasted time, lost sales, or increased taxes impact profitability? My guess is that fewer than one in fifty have that understanding in an average corporation. If you aspire eventually to leadership responsibility, can you see the value in understanding all of the factors that can impact profitability?

Two reports you should understand are the balance sheet and the income statement.

The Balance Sheet. The *balance sheet* reflects all the possessions and financial commitments of the organization. The value of the possessions are listed in a column on the left-hand side (or top) of your balance sheet and are referred to as *assets*. Included among the assets are the categories of *receivables*, *inventory* (i.e., *materials*, *work in progress*, and *finished goods*), *property*, *plant*, *deferred taxes*, *equipment*, and *other assets*. Other assets include long term investments, intangibles, and the like.

The financial commitments of a firm are referred to as *liabilities* and *owner's equity* and are listed in the right-hand column of the balance sheet. Liabilities include *accounts payable*, *notes payable*, and *long-term debt*. Accounts payable include all amounts owed to suppliers for goods they have supplied to your organization. This includes not only materials and components that your firm uses in the manufacture of products for sale but also other items such as office supplies, property taxes, and utility bills. Notes payable and long-term debt result from loans your organization has taken.

An important section of the balance sheet is *owner's equity*, the financial commitment of a firm to its owners. Equity includes all *preferred stock*, *common stock* and all *retained earnings*. Collectively, these items reflect the original investment in the company as well as subsequent income retained in the firm (not paid out as dividends) rather than distributed as dividends.

The right and left columns of the balance sheet are each totaled at the bottom, and the total of all assets is equal to the total of all liabilities and equity. This remains true, even though total company worth varies from year to year. No matter how well or how poorly a business may do, assets will be equal in value to liabilities plus equity.

As a business grows from year to year, its growth is reflected on the balance sheet. New buildings, equipment, and inventory show up as increased assets; additional loans show up as increased liabilities until the loans are paid off; and the remainder is reflected as increased owners' equity. Percentages and ratios are often used in discussing financial issues. However, with the balance sheet and the income statement as well, all entries are in dollars.

The Income Statement. The financial activities of a firm must be measured and reported periodically. Weekly, monthly, quarterly, and annual reports are used to document such things as sales, expenses, margins, and profits. Although a variety of reports are used to track various components of financial performance, the *income statement* offers the most complete overview of business activity by summarizing all revenues and expenses of an organization during a specified time period. The most common period is one year—specifically, the fiscal year. It is a basis for paying taxes and for reporting annually to the shareholders. It is also a basis for making management decisions. At the top of the income statement is business income, or *sales*. Other sources of income may include investment income (interest and dividends), rental income, or royalties.

In business, as with personal finances, there are usually more ways to spend money than there are to make it. The remaining entries on the income statement show how the money is spent by the organization and what money remains after all financial commitments have been met. The first category of expenditure is referred to as the *cost of goods sold* (CGS). CGS is what the business pays for manufacturing and material costs for goods sold during the period. CGS is deducted from sales on the income statement to determine *gross margin*. Gross margin, just like sales and CGS, is measured in dollars.

Gross margin is not the same as profit. The company has a number of other financial commitments to meet before profit is determined. Out of gross margin comes all the expenses for running the business, called *operating expenses*. Operating expenses include advertising and promotion, salaries and benefits, data processing, insurance, office supplies and equipment, postage, property taxes, rental and loan payments, social security taxes, transportation, and utilities. All these operating expenses must be deducted from the gross margin; and what remains is called *earnings*. Earnings are the basis for paying federal, state, and local income taxes. The remainder when the taxes are paid is *profit*.

The income statement provides a clear view on how much money your organization has to work with, how the money is spent, and how much is left over to return to the owners.

Market

In all likelihood, the past ten years has brought dramatic changes in the nature of your customers, competition, and/or product. Although this may seem a cliche, such changes have almost certainly resulted in structural changes in the organization—jobs added and deleted, management and policy changes, and perhaps a range of new initiatives relating to performance, quality, inventory control, and customer service. The drivers that imposed these changes probably include pricing constraints, customer demands for improved service, international competition, regulatory constraints, cost of capital, and economic conditions.

You might wonder what changes are presently occurring that will modify your business operation five years from now. How will these changes affect your department? You may not get all the answers you want, but in pursuing these questions, you will come to understand the business of your employer much better.

Contacts

Interface with capable people who have different experiences and responsibilities than you. It may be difficult to approach other departments with a lot of questions about their operation, but once you have established your intent to make a positive contribution and avoid unnecessary mistakes, you will find that others will be helpful. For example, if you need to get a drawing change approved, walk the drawing around in person and create the opportunities to ask questions. You might also ask with whom else you should meet to further your knowledge of the business.

Service and professional organizations are an effective avenue for reaching out. I recently was told of a new hire who had volunteered to organize an upcoming engineering society meeting that his company was to host. His task was to arrange for a speaker, prepare a program agenda, and arrange refreshments and publicity. He had been with the company, a Fortune 500 firm, for about three months when he assumed this task. He put the meeting together with great care, and the event proceeded without a hitch. It happened that two vice presidents were at this meeting, and one commented to the other about the quality of preparation that was evident. They sought out the individual and learned that he was a new hire. As a result, they not only introduced themselves and expressed appreciation, they both came to take a personal interest in the development of this new hire, who already had shown himself to be one who could get a job done right.

Junior Achievement is a service organization that has chapters in most large cities, and its purpose is to help high school students gain knowledge and experience by starting and running a business. For individuals with coincident interests in service work and entrepreneurship, volunteering with Junior Achievement offers excellent opportunities to collaborate with others from industry in helping high school students develop business plans, form companies, produce a product, and pursue a profit. Typically, the volunteers have significant managerial responsibility—an excellent way to become acquainted with the issues associated with business leadership.

Policies and Practices

As you become acquainted with an organization and the people who work there, it is important to learn the procedures and practices of doing business. What processes do you need to understand? From the following partial list, select a few and walk through the steps involved, taking time to discuss the process with individuals at each step.

Accident reports
Budget submittal and approval
Contract approval
Drawing/design changes
Equipment maintenance
Expense reports
Inspection reports
Personnel requisition
Preventive maintenance procedures
Procedure changes
Proposal development
Publications development
Purchase orders
Request for quotes
Travel authorization

Relevant Literature

In addition to reading literature specifically related to your functional responsibilities, keep current with professional magazines (i.e., ASME, IEEE, etc.), trade magazines, and business literature. My personal preferences for business literature include periodicals such as *Business Week* and the *Wall Street Journal*.

An Ounce of Prevention

Although the possibilities for career-related problems seem endless at times, most are easily avoidable.

Associating with the Wrong People

Avoid the negative people of the world and gravitate toward those who have a positive attitude, are respected for their integrity, and understand the business.

Attitude Problems

Now is a good time for you to act like an adult, control your feelings, and consider the others with whom you work. In addition to communications skills, perhaps the largest differentiator between true leaders and the rest is the ability to squelch negative emotions before they become destructive. A poor attitude toward management will isolate you from the organization and force management to look elsewhere for the assistance they need. Cultivate and maintain an enthusiasm for facing the needs of your management.

Failing to Communicate

Your written and oral communications show others how you think and what you know. Given that the nature of communications in the corporate world differ significantly from that in the academic environment, assume that your writing, speaking, and listening skills all require improvement. Each letter you write can be the basis for someone else to judge your abilities to analyze, plan, communicate, and take action. Once an adverse judgment is made regarding these characteristics in you, time, effort, and luck are required to effect a reversal.

You will recognize progress when others want you to write a

letter, generate a report, or give a presentation. Several useful resources are identified in Appendix B.

Germann and Arnold (1980) discuss twelve rules to be followed in your career. My comments are presented in italics:

1. Start each day's work with a smile; maintain good health, an attractive appearance, and a positive attitude. *A successful career involves the support of many people. Satisfying this rule will encourage others to offer their support and provide you the fortitude to capitalize on this support. Except for medical assistance, you have only yourself to draw upon in satisfying this rule.*

2. Take the initiative in treating others as you would like to be treated. *The "golden rule" is stressed for its proactive potential. Although working relationships in industry are generally of a "reserved" nature, try to overcome tendencies toward shyness. The professional bonds you establish with your peers and management depend largely upon the initiatives you have taken.*

3. Know your organization's goals and purposes so you can align your efforts with those of your employer. *The effectiveness with which needs and objectives are communicated can vary considerably across organizations and among management. You may need to accommodate a lack of effectiveness so that you can best align your efforts with their needs.*

4. Study the successful people in your organization. Seek their advice. *You will come to understand better the concept and value of success, and your progress in that direction will be more certain if you follow the right paradigm.*

5. Take time to consider problems before taking action. Avoid instant emotional reactions. *Finding a way to save effort while identifying a better solution requires enough time at the start to consider fully the problem, various approaches to its resolution, and their ramifications. Leaders are expected to think first before acting.*

6. Never present a problem without suggesting a construc-

tive solution. *At the heart of this is whether you will be perceived as a source of problems or progress.*

7. Communicate your contributions and accomplishments to your employer. *Recognize the contributions of others. Your management may be sufficiently busy that it is difficult for them to keep your responsibilities and progress in proper perspective. A year-end report offers good opportunity for reviewing your progress. I believe these communications ought to be balanced, defensible, and devoid of "fluff." Learn to acknowledge the contributions of others in making progress toward goals. Avoid generalizations and undefensible claims that can undermine the factual content of your report.*

8. Establish a reputation for doing your assignments well and on time. *Far too many deadlines are missed. As a manager, I found such delays extremely annoying, yet more frequent than they should have been. It is easy for management to label a person who misses schedule commitments as undependable.*

9. When you are in control of your job, add new responsibility with your superior's agreement. *You will increase your value as a resource to your employer, and your responsibilities may become more inspiring.*

10. Plan the next step in your job and career. Never be without achievable goals. *I tend to think of this less in terms of ladder-climbing and more in the sense of increased abilities, knowledge, and flexibility for the individual.*

11. Continue your formal or informal education; never stop learning and growing. *At a point when I was promoted to manager, I also found myself sitting on a fairly active school board. The contrast in management styles and strategic thinking offered me a wonderful view. I repeatedly learned a successful approach in one arena that were subsequently found useful in the other.*

12. Continue building and communicating with your contact network. *Remember, they are not contacts, they are people. People are more interesting than contacts.*

It is obvious that I am in close agreement with these recommendations of Germann and Arnold (1980). Their book, *Job and Career Building*, is comprehensive and relevant to a large audience.

What Do Other New Hires Say?

In the previously mentioned survey of individuals taken during the first five years of their careers (graduating classes of 1986 through 1991; see Appendix A), almost all responses were offered within the context of change from college to career.

Notable among the results are the coincident establishment of clear career goals with the accrual of experience, the evolving definition of success from fame and fortune to competence and contribution, and the general sense of mission that seemed to permeate the 245 responses. The questionnaire was composed of two kinds of questions. One set of questions sought feedback that could be easily quantified (multiple choice, ranking, and short answer), and a corresponding set allowed the respondent to express opinions and observations regarding career-related issues in a more open format. Both sets of questions yielded considerable information for analysis.

Setting and Meeting Goals

As may be expected, work experience had a penetrating influence on recent graduates. Only one-third of the respondents had specific career goals during their senior-year job search, but within a year or two of experience, three-quarters of the respondents had such goals. Only two individuals had backtracked from having clear career goals at graduation to having none currently.

The following comments confirm the role played by experience and the effect of having clear goals:

> *Realize through work what one likes or dislikes.*
>
> *Have become more focused, yet more realistic.*
>
> *Experience has led to goals.*
>
> *Job has changed goal—clearer views.*
>
> *Been following goals, knew what I wanted and went after it.*

   Without doubt, a clear goal is a prerequisite for motivation,
but how do you better define your career goals? As noted next,
experience is a prerequisite. The challenge for the college graduate is to find their entry point onto the career growth cycle (Figure 4.1). Common recommendations volunteered on our survey
responses included:

> *Get experience to determine your goals.*
> *Research companies and get counseling.*
> *Make contacts in your area of interest.*
> *Be open-minded.*
> *Determine what you want and go after it.*
> *Learn as much as possible.*
> *Make sure you're happy.*
> *Talk to alumni.*

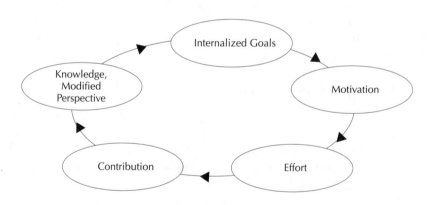

Fig. 4.1   The managed track of career experience.

   It is reassuring to note that 94 percent of those who responded
indicated that they were making progress toward career goals.
This seems to highlight the dilemma of the college senior trying
to articulate a clear set of career objectives before acquiring sufficient industrial responsibility and exposure. Curiously, this 94
percent making progress toward clear goals exceeds the 75 percent who currently have clear goals!

Getting the Job, Getting the Promotion

Recent graduates indicate that motivation is the most important trait their employer seeks when recruiting talent. A willingness to learn, communications skills, confidence, punctuality, independence, and being well-rounded are also considered critical. When measuring job performance, most employers emphasize productivity and responsibility, recent graduates note. Additional areas of importance included judgment, teamwork, profitability, leadership, and accuracy of work.

To Do or Not to Do

What can get in the way of a successful career or job start? What should be done once clear goals are established? The do's and don't's are listed here:

Successful Career Starts

What Works	What Doesn't Work
Commit to goals	Bad attitude
Be open-minded and confident	Poor motivation/not aggressive
Work hard, do your best	Poor economic conditions
Utilize contacts; network	Close-mindedness
Go after dreams	The wrong job
Enjoy life and have fun	Personal limitations/ inflexibility
Don't limit yourself	Inability—poor experience/ skills/training
Don't fear change	Lack of mentor/no direction
Be selective	Uncaring boss
Take risks and be flexible	Not having goals
Be candid/honest	Tardiness/missed deadlines

Flexibility at Work

Nine out of ten respondents placed importance on job and/or career flexibility. Fortunately, the average respondent felt a moderate to strong degree of flexibility in his or her current position. When asked to describe the nature of flexibility, alumni offered the following representative comments:

> *Qualified for multiple/changing job roles*
> *Broad responsibilities and experience*
> *Control over career path*
> *Adaptability to new situations and people*
> *Willingness to develop and try other functions*

There was a positive correlation among individuals who valued flexibility, who saw career-related stress as a positive motivator, and who felt a sense of progress toward their career goals.

Career Satisfaction

Most survey responses included extensive feedback regarding career satisfaction. The results of most and least satisfying aspects of a job are listed here (the most frequent responses are at top):

Most Satisfying Aspects	Least Satisfying Aspects
Knowledge gained	Corporate politics
Sense of contribution/ responsibility	Negative co-workers
Helping customers/ benefiting others	Hours on the job
Teamwork	Economy/layoffs
Job independence	Low sense of worth
Challenge	Stress/pressure
Problem solving/ decision making	Limited growth opportunity
Constant change/diversity	Paperwork/tedium
Meeting objectives	Financial reward
Financial reward	Routine

The definition of success seems to evolve significantly from college to the career environment. Although it seems easy to revert to money and position as accepted indicators of success, once the professional career commences, a change in perspective seems to tie career success more closely with personal contribution to the success of the organization and the environment. The most frequently cited components of career success (descending order) included are as follows:

1. Personal happiness
2. Job satisfaction
3. Responsibility and contribution
4. Financial reward
5. Right balance in life
6. Challenge
7. Upward mobility
8. Meeting personal goals
9. Learning
10. Meeting career goals
11. Realizing personal growth

Job Related Stress

Individuals were asked if they considered their responsibilities to be stressful. Also, their views were sought regarding whether stress has a positive or a negative role in their careers.

In general, most felt that their responsibilities are quite stressful but were divided in their opinions of stress as a positive influence in their personal careers. Although divided on the question of stress, the aggregate response identified stress as being a slightly positive factor in personal and professional development. I believe that those who felt stress was a positive influence had associated it with learning, growth, and attainment of objectives, whereas the others saw it more as an impediment to their development. Of course, there are numerous forms and causes of stress, many of which are, indeed, negative influences. My interest was to consider those that are work-related.

When the possibility of important correlations among the question responses was considered, one finding stood out. The individual's perception of stress as a positive influence in his or her career correlates with several important factors.

Individuals perceiving stress as a positive or constructive element in their work are much more likely to have done the following:

Established career goals.

Made progress toward goals.

Valued a sense of contribution at work.

Have a sense of flexibility in their work.

Have entrepreneurial plans and/or accomplishments.

This finding should encourage recent graduates to accept challenge more readily and expect that reasonable challenges will aid them in their professional growth.

Changing Jobs and Relocation

Of those surveyed, the average respondent had graduated $3^1/_2$ years earlier and had changed companies one time. It was not surprising that one in six of the respondents were actively seeking to change employers.

Relocation can be a sticking point with many college seniors for a variety of reasons, yet the experience of relocating, once accomplished, is perceived as a strongly positive one. Later, having children in school, a second career in the household, or other important family or personal ties can all add significantly to the challenges of uprooting to a new location. However, economic conditions and opportunities seem to be regionally fluid, thus offering an almost ever-present incentive to consider relocation. Thus, a choice of home is not simple at graduation; it becomes increasingly complex as family and personal commitments evolve, yet the stability of maintaining roots in one location seems less likely than ever.

Survey results were evenly divided as to the personal importance of location in pursuing a career opportunity. Of the 186 respondents who did relocate from their college and home towns, 96 percent indicated that the experience of relocation was a strongly positive one, even though some noted that relocation was not easy.

Graduate Studies

The pursuit of graduate studies was considered moderately important (scale choices included none, slight, moderate, and strong), but 87 percent indicated that work experience should precede the pursuit of graduate studies.

Almost three-fourths of the recent graduates in our study plan to or have completed graduate work, and another 7 percent consider it a possibility (Figure 4.2). It was recommended by 87 percent that graduate school be deferred until several years after graduation to gain experience. With many, the initial work responsibilities clarified the value and direction of study, and for some, graduate study offered a change in direction toward management or law, for example. It was the exception, but a few respondents noted that experience swayed them against graduate studies; they were optimistic about the opportunities they had and wished to focus their career growth efforts on the job.

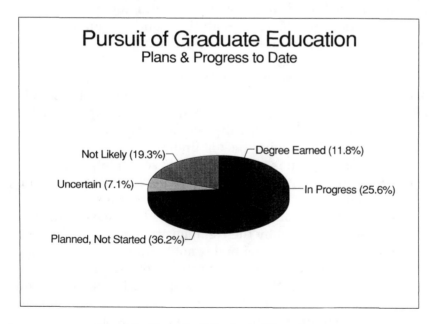

Fig. 4.2 Pursuit of Graduate Education

Why pursue a graduate degree? It can provide additional breadth, greater depth, or a shift in focus. The master of business administration (MBA) offers a broad exposure to business-related topics and thus can complement the undergraduate engineering curriculum content. Because many engineers in industry eventually assume managerial responsibilities, this would seem to make sense. A master of science in management can offer exposure similar to that of the MBA, but it allows the engineer to focus on a specific area of business such as project management, finance, or the management of technology.

A MS or ME in engineering provides the opportunity to explore a topic in considerable depth and is also an effective approach for shifting career focus. The engineer who currently works on power supplies, for example, can use a graduate program to establish ability in controls engineering if he or she wishes to proceed in that direction.

In the United States in particular, individuals have the good fortune of being able to change career direction significantly. A budding electrical engineer can, for example, pursue a career change that will lead to law, environmental engineering, medicine, education, or science, and all these options can be pursued directly at the graduate level. Most nonengineers do not have this flexibility.

One reason not to pursue a degree is simply because it looks good or because it is the path of least resistance. Students too often attend graduate school immediately after completing a baccalaureate program because they do not know what they want and thus defer the tougher task of finding a job.

Another decision is whether to go to school full time or part time. Part-time programs can often be persued in the evening, allowing individuals to maintain their current job responsibilities while earning money and probably to have most college-related expenses covered by their employers. Such a course poses difficulties in that the individual is not allowed to immerse himself or herself in the educational process, education competes for time and attention with both family and work-related commitments, and it usually takes longer to meet degree requirements.

Full-time students are able to concentrate on their studies and research and may be more likely to receive funding support for their education from the university or a sponsored professor. Full-time study can allow individuals to step away from industry for a few years to rethink their career plans and approach their careers with a fresh start as they near the completion of their graduate work. Being a full-time student allows utilization of the college placement service and affords the time to conduct a more concerted job search effort. More time accommodates travel for interviews and allows investigating career opportunities in other industries. Some may argue that full-time programs tend to be stronger; you will have to decide which programs best meet your needs and what sacrifices you can afford in pursuing the program of your choice.

It is clear that recent graduates give their careers considerable thought and willingly share their views and experiences. The transition from student to employee begins at the beginning of the senior year of college and continues for several years into the work experience. At the time of graduation, the senior is "neither here nor there" but is in the midst of a struggle both to initiate and to cope with change.

A lack of experience makes it difficult to obtain good experience—a Catch 22 that also hampers your ability to identify personal career goals. Because there is a lack of work experience, most individuals tend to develop career goals after some experience is garnered. Once started in their careers, a significant majority of respondents expressed a sense of progress in their personal or career growth.

Coincident with evolving career goals is often a change in the definition of success. Students are likely to lack a clear, workable definition of career success and satisfaction. A more tangible definition, which often comes to include competence, contribution to the organization, growth in abilities and responsibility, and flexibility as the important components, evolves in the workplace. This evolving definition serves to motivate the individual toward larger responsibilities and greater contributions.

If your job was easy, then anyone could do it, and you would not have needed to spend four years in college. The difficulties of your job responsibilities, coupled with your need to maintain an adequate cash flow, dictate that your career will not only be a source of money and opportunity but will also be a source of stress. As we have noted with José and Susan, the initial years replaced one set of problems with another as each gained experi-

ence and authority. The initial communication problems and lack
of apparent career progress are supplanted by new communications problems and new threats to career progress.

One important difference between experienced and inexperienced employees is how unseasoned employees approach their
challenges. Recent graduates may tend to address these stresses
emotionally, which is bad because it frequently degrades further
the ability of a new employee to communicate effectively with
management due to a growing mistrust. The most pronounced
difference between the capable manager and the inexperienced
and perhaps immature employee appears in his or her reaction
to this stress. The immature reaction is to personalize situations.
This, of course, hampers the ability to work and to communicate
effectively. In this mode it is, of course, difficult to realize significant progress toward career goals. More-seasoned employees,
who are making good progress with their careers are better able
to depersonalize problems that cause stress. In this way, they
are more able to address the problems and identify solutions that
are mutually beneficial to the organization as well as the individual.

Those who viewed job-related stress as a positive influence
were more likely to have goals, be entrepreneurial, be making
progress toward goals, and place importance on their ability to
make a contribution.

In Their Words

*Work very hard—harder than anyone else. Take your work very
seriously. Don't think you're at work to make friends and have fun.
Develop a reputation early as someone who is reliable and gets the
job done. Be your boss's "right-hand person."*

*Put your whole-hearted effort into what you want, but be patient if
things do not happen overnight. Progress takes time. I believe the
saying "good things come to those who wait" is true.*

*Obtain opinions from many about how to build a career; keep an
open mind and consider many options (there is more than one route
to travel on a journey); communicate clearly your goals to management; ask for and use feedback; start careers 'hot' to take advantage of the power of first impressions; stay balanced—there is more
to life than work.*

Leave room in your definition so that you are not working for a goal with blinders on. As the old saying goes, "the fun is not arriving at your destination, but it is the trip getting there." By keeping your eyes open along the way, you are able to enjoy the trip more and take advantage of opportunities that may occur. All in all, seek a career that will give you pleasure.

I would consider the first two years out of college to be a trial-and-error period. Never be afraid to move laterally or to try a new position. There is more than one road to success. I feel a college graduate may think he or she has a well-defined career goal, but without professional experience in the corporate world, one can be misled in a particular career path.

Nothing is set in stone—your "well-defined career goals" might sound good when you graduate but might not fulfill you personally, only professionally. Do not be afraid to change your direction—after all, Sam Walton of Walmart didn't open his first store until he was 46 years old!

Do not have an attitude that you are too good or too educated— essentially over-qualified to perform a particular job or task. You may hate it, but it pays off—doing grunt work sometimes. Everyone has had to do it at some point in his or her career. It shows you are willing to help out and are a team player, and, believe it or not, people will respect you more in the long run.

Follow your dreams at all costs—no matter what you do, if you really enjoy it and believe in it, you will be able to support yourself doing it and will probably be very successful at it. Never listen to people who say that your career goals are unattainable or that you are making the wrong decision—they are only jealous that you have the strength to follow your dreams.

Take life one day at a time, but always have an idea where you want to be in the future. Don't wish away tomorrow, because time flies. Always keep an open mind on jobs and an updated résumé, because no matter what level you are on within a company, things can change in a second. If you change companies, never burn the bridge between yourself and the previous employer.

It is not enough to consider the environment of change from the graduate's perspective. His or her manager is also critical to the success of a career; the manager has needs as well. It is necessary to consider what might be said to and about management.

Chapter 5

Opportunities for Management to Help New Employees

Few things help an individual
more than to place responsibility
upon him, and to let him know
that you trust him.

Booker T. Washington

You may be a "captain of industry" now, but you probably started your career as a grunt and encountered your share of early-career anxieties. You doubtless experienced a failure or two, but perhaps you had the perseverance to learn from mistakes and proceed with the responsibilities given to you. The commencement of your career probably generated many vivid memories. Some problems may have been formative in your career development, just as, for example, falling off of a bicycle or touching a hot stove were to your childhood. You learned to recognize and avoid situations at work that make you particularly uncomfortable. Nobody wants to be a grunt for very long, and you worked very hard to increase your control over your destiny. Your desires and efforts to see your career grow into greener pastures proceeded with a testing of where the fences were as you sought a path of growth. Your agility for finding a path of progress while avoiding shocks grew as you approached the greener pastures of management. You avoided a lot of shocks and remained successful in your pursuits of growth.

GEE WHIZ, YOU CAN'T FIND A GOOD BOSS ANYMORE.

Having arrived at the wheel, you may find yourself more alone in your responsibilities than you anticipated. At the middle and lower levels of the organization, it seemed as if the boss usually had good information and a solid understanding of business operation, regardless of how complex the operation was. From below, poor business decisions appeared to be only judgmental error on the boss's part rather than a result of misleading or incomplete information being channeled to upper management. You certainly did not expect to be forced to question the content and spin of all information and advice you are given, regardless of whether its source is internal or external to the organization. Because of this, you may sometimes feel as if you are looking at the operation through a haze—it is with great difficulty that you discern the information needed to avoid the icebergs that lurk throughout your operating environment. You are surprised both at the resources you have and the resources you lack for making important strategic decisions and recognize that others will question your decision-making abilities at one time or another.

Also, although you have held a number of positions that you have greatly enjoyed over the years, you now find that you like being captain best of all. Becoming captain required hard work, some successful projects, and certainly some good luck, but never have you had a greater opportunity to make a contribution to the business than by focusing the efforts of a good organization. More than ever, you are depended upon for your ability to think and communicate. You find the demands of your responsibilities stimulating, and the opportunity is at hand to draw upon your experience and knowledge to form creative growth plans.

IT TAKES TWO TO GROW A CAREER

Alas, there are obstacles you must overcome to realize the accomplishments that you see are possible:

1. There is a lack of knowledge among middle- and lower-level employees as to how the business operates, what characterizes success, and how decisions are made.
2. There is a reluctance for individuals at all levels to address problems before they are elevated to the next higher level of management.
3. Few understand what information you need and what information you do not need.

As a result of these obstacles, your organization continually forces you to be far more reactive than you want to be. You will be unable to define a future for the business until you can get your subordinates coping effectively with today's problems. You may have to start with your own vice presidents to implement the philosophical changes desired. You must demand that your organization address business issues effectively at the lowest possible level. Even the recruiting and indoctrination of new hires must be accomplished with this in mind; it is your only hope for realizing your goals for the business development.

Perhaps you can kill a few birds with one stone and get a large part of your organization out of the grunt mode. If so, your employees will be better able to help free you so you can address important business issues and thus become a more effective strategist (and feel less lonely). Before you consider a plan of action, consider the operating environment in which you compete.

Your Challenges and Your Need for New Talent

A number of changes now occurring in industry collectively pave a path toward increased business sophistication and, one hopes, business growth. Quality improvement and total quality processes, inventory management, financial management, and business consolidation all offer examples of significant change. However, this preponderance of concepts, knowledge, and advice is a double-edged sword.

On the positive side, essential factors such as customer service, inventory optimization, financial strategy, integrated manufacturing, and cost controls receive close attention. Such attention has resulted primarily from increased customer demands for service and quality and from the ever-present technology, quality, and cost constraints imposed by your competition. These market-drivers have been intensified by the computerization of data bases, communications, and business performance analysis. Once a practice of large companies only, computerization can now be implemented effectively by the smallest family businesses. Industry meets this squeeze with improved quality, improved efficiency, and the availability of more accurate and timely information. These are the elements of business success at year-end. It cannot be overlooked that increased regulatory, legal, and health care—related costs have impeded growth and financial performance. In spite of improvements in operational efficiency and information management, the larger portion of gain has arguably been eaten up by this increased overhead.

The immediacy of information and control, together with the burden of increased regulatory and risk-management constraints, force business to reach a much higher level of operational efficiency—and not always with commensurate increases in profit. The challenge for many firms is to become stable or even survive.

Reduced transaction times for information and response thwart long-term strategy. Today, it is possible for business organizations to be so focused on specific approaches to near-term goals and needs, such as year-end reporting, that you, as a business leader, are distracted in efforts to maintain long-range vision and strategy. In fact, I believe that many organizations in U.S. industry have been broadly, but adversely, impacted by the preponderance and popularity of new "improvement" programs. A quest for increased competitiveness becomes a siren to embrace the latest buzz words and follow the most recently heralded corporate gurus in a variety of corporate betterment programs. The disturbance created by these programs, in the wrong hands, can disrupt fundamental business decision-making processes by interjecting unproductive distractions. Without proper controls implemented, a new developmental program can take your most expensive and most needed leaders out of commission for a seemingly endless series of meetings. Long-range planning efforts are often subject to such waste. It is difficult to argue against the need for a long-range plan, yet most efforts fail to include adequate accountability. The frustration is evident among employees after considerable time and money have been spent on vision and mission statements, which too often fail to influence business decision making. Isn't it interesting that the concept of accountability is almost always associated with short-term performance only? Thus, the current market dynamics dictate that you are largely reactive in your leadership. You can do better than this, but there are precious few visible examples for you to follow.

There is something that is much more scarce, something rarer than ability. It is the ability to recognize ability.
                                        Robert Half

The challenge of strategic business planning and development is further complicated by market dynamics. The form and function of successful manufacturing in fifteen years is difficult to accurately project—you may have said as much yourself. One expects that some of the currently recognized leaders will be displaced and that others will rise as a result of creative and effective product development, process improvement, marketing, and development of resources. This changing of the guard may show itself in abrupt steps rather than through gradual evolution. Instead, profound structural changes in the role and manner of employment in our culture will greatly affect individual perceptions regarding work. The advent of new industry leaders is often distracting in and of itself. An organization may find it easier to follow a Japanese or Walmart management model rather than maintain a basic and effective understanding of its company's health.

A look at the recent past offers a hint of the possible changes when we consider at interest rates, inflation, the Persian Gulf, the communist block failure and subsequent instability, health care issues, defense cuts, and the free-trade agreements. These fundamental forces impact the economy and culture of industry. If your organization is fully occupied with the immediacy of customers' needs and if the crystal ball looks cloudy after the next six months, what is to be done for the long haul?   In my opinion, there really are only two steps that most organizations can take.

Presumably, you have the first step well in hand: maintaining the financial and market viability of your business, which includes customer satisfaction, efficient financial and logistical management, operational flexibility, micromarket attention to sales and margin across the board, and, of course, doing it all right the first time—quality. Performing these functions well contributes greatly to good customer relations, profitability, and the resulting financial strength. Everybody wants financial strength, but a war chest of net worth is an absolute necessity for weathering economic and market storms. Money buys time— time you will need for achieving the organizational and operational changes required to accommodate new market structures.

The second step is the recruitment and development of talent. The increasing ability of your employees to think and grow with your business will help you face the economic and market storms encountered. Most companies fail to do this well because their attention is on the functional skills that meet their near-term needs (i.e., design, testing, manufacturing, sales, accounting, and marketing). Employees are not sensitized to the larger issues of change around them, and they are not encouraged to contemplate and participate in serious long-range strategic planning. I have found precious few organizations where the majority of salaried personnel maintain a solid understanding of business performance. Can you imagine a professional ball player not knowing his batting average or team standing?

The company that grows to assume a leadership role in its industry will do so only because its employees understand and accommodate change in technology and markets. The success stories have a foundation of thinking, participating employees. As a manager, you are accountable for the people you hire and for their development. Are your expectations high enough?

Recruiting

Interviewing college seniors may seem a lot like trying to negotiate a contract in a foreign language—it is a test of communications skills. Even when agreement is reached, it is unlikely that both parties see the agreement the same way. Your problem with hiring recent graduates seems to be that they do not know what you need, they do not yet know how to do the job, they expect too much (i.e., growth, responsibility, and compensation), and they cannot communicate effectively. They are more likely to make a commitment that subsequently makes them uncomfortable, and it is easier for you to reflect upon their shortcomings rather than on your own. For these reasons, many companies prefer to recruit only experienced individuals and will not consider hiring recent graduates. Unfortunately, many firms have yet to realize the opportunity in and assume the responsibility of initiating co-op work/study programs as a means of aiding and evaluating the best developing talent.

Why bother recruiting college seniors? In general, engineering graduates possess a good work ethic, they are educated *and* trainable. Sometimes overlooked but perhaps most important of all, they hold high expectations for their lives and their careers. Those values offer you incredible potential for developing great talent.

Companies recruit seniors in a variety of ways. Having been on both sides of the fence and on top of it (job hunting, recruiting, and teaching/advising), I find the on-campus recruiting view to be most fascinating. Some companies seem to project an outstanding image as a prospective employer, and others show genuine ability for screening candidates and regularly selecting individuals who subsequently perform extremely well for them. It has not been obvious to me that one group of recruiters is related to the other.

Li-Weng Chang graduated three years ago and was eager to return to his alma mater. He was proud to be working for one of the county's largest companies and looked forward to playing the role of recruiter. In fact, Li-Weng lobbied hard to be placed on the recruiting travel schedule. He has worked in a design department, but his company HR department has prepped him in interviewing techniques, and he was somewhat aware of the legal limits to the questions he could ask in the interview. He had a full schedule for two days of interviewing and was part of a team of recruiters (who were all conducting interviews). His company held an evening informational meeting for the students to dispense with the preliminary questions. The company was a household name, and they had no problem with name recognition on campus. A majority of the students found the company presentation and video tape encouraging. At the evening's informational meeting, Li-Weng was introduced, but the presentation was naturally given by the senior team members. Over the next two days, Li-Weng interviewed twenty-six seniors.

His design responsibilities over the past three years were exciting for him, but his exposure to other opportunities and career paths was quite limited. Li-Weng felt that the company should hire only engineers and thought that mechanical engineers were not quite as capable as electrical and chemical engineers. After the interviews were complete, the views of Li-Weng's candidates regarding employment opportunities seemed to differ from those who interviewed with other recruiters. Li-Weng was new in this position of authority and was anxious to present himself as a successful graduate.

Unfortunately, Li-Weng was perceived by several as the company's definition of success, and they did not find this to be attractive. Several candidates were disappointed that they had not interviewed with someone more broadly experienced in the organization. Candidates wanted to learn about the wide range of design and manufacturing activities that might be available to pursue, and they would have appreciated an interviewer able to take a more active interest in individual candidates. Li-Weng recommended only a few students for a job trip. Of those, few second interviews yielded results.

There were other interviewers for the same company. Lora Kulakowski had about fifteen years of experience and was currently a marketing manager with one of the commercial electronic business units. She would never have predicted that she would assume marketing responsibilities, but her engineering experience gave her a good product and customer background. Although all her professional experience was with the same company, it ranged from design to project management to sales. Lora had interviewed before and looked forward to her college visits. She had not attended this college, but previous recruiting visits here had been enjoyable and quite successful for her. Lora had recruited several members of her department from this institution. Being from the south, she enjoyed a rare opportunity to stay over and watch a good hockey team. As with Li-Weng, Lora had a full two days of interviewing.

Lora wanted every interview to count. Perhaps there were one or two exceptions where a student seemed to be unreachable, but she had resolved to accomplish three goals during each interview, as long as she had the student's cooperation:

- *Make a customer.* Lora was a believer in her employer and its products, and she wanted the candidate to like her company. Preferably, Lora wanted them to be attracted to the good opportunities that she knew existed, but if not, she also wanted them to view her company and its engineering as being the best available.

- *Determine what the candidate really wanted in a job.* This goal was not easy to fulfill. For one thing, usually the résumé's objective statement was not only not helpful; it was misleading. Second, she found that many students were initially reluctant to discuss the aspects of a career that they might really look forward to. Once a bond of trust was established however, those candidates tended to become more open in sharing their likes and dislikes with Lora. This allowed Lora to confirm or correct the candidate's stated career objective and perhaps identify other kinds of opportunities that many students are unaware of.

- *Help the individual's career search, even if it led away from Lora's company.* Achieving this result meant providing feedback on interviewing, offering suggestions for how the candidate might be most successful in pursuing opportunities with Lora's employer, or, whenever necessary, identifying opportunities with other companies and industries. Lora intended that the candidate recognize that she and her employer were working for the well-being of the individual.

With very few exceptions, Lora's interviews went well, and she usually made good progress toward meeting her objectives. The company does not track the performance of individual interviewers, but Lora had a fair idea what the results were. On average, she might have a few more candidates get job trips, but year after year, twice as many of her recommended candidates were extended offers. She took pleasure in being able to help both her company and college seniors find what they were looking for. Each year several college placement offices were encouraged to note her name on the list of visiting recruiters.

As the recruiting effort passes from the hiring phase to getting new employees up to a functioning level, the responsibility is passed from management to supervision. What happens?

The pyramid shown in Figure 5.1 represents the hierarchy of activity for the new employee. At the base are the required coverage of rules, regulations, standard procedures, organization charts, benefits, and so on. Through classroom sessions and required reading programs, the human resources department ushers the new employee through the necessary indoctrination. The

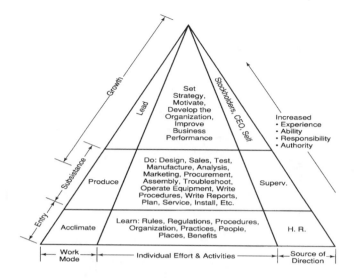

Fig. 5.1   Hierarchy of Activity for the New Employee

employee's supervisor has little to do with this aspect of his or her development, other than allowing the employee time away from office responsibilities to attend class sessions. The supervisor's accountability is for the next level—getting work done.

The Role of Supervision

The supervisors' unique responsibility in the organization is to see that specific tasks get done on time, that individuals in their group know how to do the necessary work, and that everyone keeps busy. Supervisors are the larger interface between the organization and the individual.

Supervisors can be at somewhat of a disadvantage in their responsibilities. On occasion, they may be used by management to maintain distance from individual employees, or they may themselves be somewhat isolated from larger organizational issues. This increases their difficulty in aiding the development of new employees. Although the role of first-line supervision regarding employee development varies considerably from company to company, I believe it is necessary for the supervisor to be the primary driver in helping employees and management develop mutual understanding and respect. The organization must find

CAREER OBJECTIVES? DON'T NEED THEM.NOW,
I ALREADY HAVE A JOB.

a way for the supervisor to facilitate communications among management and new employees. You will see that this is not so difficult. It is possible to develop supervision and new hires simultaneously.

Getting New Hires on Line

The supervisor's immediate task is to help the new employee attain a minimum set of standards, thus enabling the individual to perform useful work. The new hire is introduced to the other members of the department and is encouraged to start learning about various responsibilities. Assignments are given to the employee that will probably result in his or her seeking assistance as required and gaining knowledge.

Once the employee has reached a minimum functioning level, he or she is able to contribute to the accomplishment of tasks and is justifying his or her position in the organization. At this point, the individual is able to blend into the organization—that is, seem less conspicuous than he or she was as a newcomer. Overcoming the entry level is a relief for the supervisor as well, allowing both supervisor and employee to become a little more comfortable. At this point, the active incentives for further employee development can become much less apparent. The efforts that helped the new hire attain the first two levels of accomplishment (indoctrination and entry-level performance) are inadequate for assisting the employee to the third level, growth beyond minimum functional requirements.

With the employee now assuming a reasonable work load, what further objectives should be met? Listed here are seven objectives for employee development; they offer a framework for evaluating developmental programs.

Increase employee contribution. This goal is an obvious one for the business, and the importance of his or her labor ought to be apparent to the employee as well. If contribution is the commodity of exchange in the workplace, its value must be commonly recognized at every level of the organization.

Improve the performance of the organization. Employees must be developed to function well as team members. This seems obvious, but often a department will stop after minimum needs have been met. In doing so, it overlooks opportunities to extend the employees' abilities, which may offer the supervisor greater flexibility in setting and meeting the departmental commitments (the benefits of meeting this objective are more apparent under dynamic circumstances—when the department's ability to meet commitments is challenged by increased work load, labor shortages, or changing departmental responsibilities). In both stable and unstable circumstances, progress here is evident in a department's effectiveness for generating presentations, reports, and proposals.

Accelerate careers. No one loses when an employee earns a higher level of ability and responsibility. Once the employee realizes that you are an advocate for his or her career growth, he or she will become more sensitized to your needs.

Reduce attrition. People leave jobs because they have an inadequate sense of role. Even though low salary is the most frequently cited cause of employees' leaving, I have found this to be only a convenient excuse, which overlooks the greater sense of self-worth that employees seek. The recognized ability to make important contributions to the group effort is essential.

Obtain direct feedback on supervisory performance. Management interface with developing employees offers feedback on supervisory performance. There are many distractions that cause this responsibility to seem less pressing than others. But as a manager, wouldn't you have a better idea of how effective your supervisors are if you personally followed the development of all new employees? Your supervisors need this support, and with your active participation, they will be more likely to involve you with questions and problems that arise.

Gain familiarity with new talent. Have you ever noticed how often others may identify an employee to you as either particularly effective or ineffective, only to have subsequent experience prove otherwise? You must find out for yourself which individuals have the growth potential for meeting your staffing needs. Likewise, those new hires need to understand that they are being followed with interest by top management. Being watched from above is a great performance incentive.

Improve good will. Companies need the full support of their people. This support must include not only active desire to contribute but active effort for the success of the organization and its members.

The value of these goals are intuitively obvious—yet they are too often missed. Success depends upon an organization's deliberate efforts to involve itself in meeting these objectives. The following plan is directed at developing the employee's ability to understand, communicate within, and contribute to your business environment. The nature of your enterprise will dictate those steps to be emphasized most.

Step 1: Product Life Consider a product that has been an important contributor to business volume. The employee should look at the history of the product from concept, through development and testing, to market entry. About how many employees worked on the product at each phase, and what is the current labor commitment to this product? Is the product profitable, and has it resulted in other new products? What is the current estimate for the remaining product life? How was engineering involved at each phase? Were there any notable problems during its development or initial market entry? Does the product result in additional sales of services or after-market needs? Has the product line been subject to any significant regulatory factors that support or impede strong market performance?

Step 2 : Engineering   The HR training program has probably acquainted new employees with an overview of corporate structure. If your firm makes robotic equipment, for example, how does the organization differentiate between and manage the mechanical, electrical, and software engineering activities? Is all design work subject to the same level and process of review? If not, what are the differences, and why do they exist? Do engineers work only in engineering? An awareness of how engineers interface among the respective activities of design, manufacturing, testing, field services, and marketing is worth covering. The new employee will be interested in examples of other engineers who have moved from one functional responsibility to another.

Step 3: Production / Manufacturing   After gaining an overview of manufacturing activities, it is worth considering how manufacturing performance is monitored and evaluated. It is likely that a significant quality thrust has occurred over the past ten years, and if flexible or cellular manufacturing techniques have been implemented, the employee should learn how they differ from the older, traditional methods. What has been the impact on expenses, quality, and profitability? Next, consider having someone walk the engineer through a recent capital project that has been completed. Who proposed the project and why? What were the necessary approvals for the project, and how much time was required to obtain them? Does this process vary much from one project to another? What possible projects are in the works now?

Step 4: Procurement   An executive in one large company,

well known for its consumer and industrial products, recently told me that sixty-two cents on every sales dollar went out of the company through procurement/purchasing. Further, the company had identified the procurement process as having the greatest potential for improving corporate financial performance. Your procurement personnel can explain the steps in completing a purchase order and give examples of problems that result from commonly made mistakes. How much is it worth to avoid one of these mistakes?

Step 5: Testing, Design Change, and Field Service With the emphasis on engineering design in the undergraduate curriculum, seniors and recent graduates are frequently unaware of the role engineers play in testing, procedure development, design changes, and field support/services (depending upon the needs of your specific industry). What causes a design to be changed, what are the necessary steps, and what do design changes cost the business in money and time? Walk the employee through several examples and acquaint him or her with some of the best and worst examples of design changes that have occurred in the past five years. What is the minimum cost and time required to have a drawing revision approved?

What does it mean to have a design or a procedure qualified? My experience was that almost two-thirds of all development costs were incurred after the initial design was completed and a prototype had been assembled. These costs included testing, modification, procedure development, and qualification.

Step 6: Customers It would be nice if your new employees could meet with a few of your representative customers and hear from them what they look for in a product. The customers should be made aware of the reasons for the meeting and recognize the opportunity for helping individuals in your organization better understand and meet their needs. What is their business, and what other kinds of products do they purchase? When they work with a supplier, what are the difficulties they want most to avoid? The employee should feel free to ask whatever questions are important, as long as the customer's time is respected. In my experience, customers will greatly appreciate your efforts to sensitize employees to customer needs.

Step 7: Sales and Competition   With an exposure to products, manufacturing, and customers, a look at the sales operation is a natural next step.   Use your sales/marketing organization to describe your business in some detail, describing how much it costs to sell a product.   Can your salespeople explain how the market has evolved over the past ten to twenty years with respect to customer base, product, price, and competition?   Because new employees cannot (and should not) talk to competitors directly, the sales operation ought to take some time to characterize product lines, reputation, and market performance of your competition.

In many organizations, proposal development is a large ongoing effort, with departments issuing several proposals a week for new work.   Let the employee see how teams are assembled to prepare a proposal and bid on a job.   Proposal development is a good task for involving the new employee; it provides an important new perspective on business operation.   It also offers an opportunity for participation in the development process and for observing the interface needed among the various departments to generate a satisfactory proposal.

Step 8: Contracts and Legal Advisement   Why does your company have standard terms and conditions for contracting with other firms, and how do they influence the necessary balance between competitiveness and security?   Once a contract is awarded, how is it administered?   Who tracks the financial and project performance, and who is responsible for ensuring that all of the terms of the contract are met?   Help your employees to understand the answers to these questions.   If you are in a heavily regulated industry, how much effort goes into government reporting?

Step 9: Marketing   How does your company study and plan for the market, and how do you sell?   What kind of people are selected for marketing responsibility; that is, should they have a technical background?   If so, how are they trained?

It is the realm of marketing operations that often generate recommendations for product revisions and new product offerings.   How do they analyze market potential?   When and how do they interface with engineering, manufacturing, and sales when the proposal of a new product arises, and who makes the decision to proceed with development?

Step 10: Heritage Company history fades quickly in the face of year-end objectives, reorganization, and merger/acquisition activity. Perhaps it is difficult for you to see the worth of having any employee review company history. I believe a sense of heritage can be an important stabilizing factor in a stormy business climate. Further, it is likely that individuals exist who held key roles and understand well the transitions experienced during the past twenty years.

I confess to being a pragmatist and concede that a knowledge of corporate history ought to be valued for the light it can shed on current business climate, decision-making activities, customer perceptions, and competitive pressures. The time may return when corporate heritage, company loyalty, and civic responsibility are broadly held in high regard.

Step 11: Meeting Management After graduation, I accepted a position in planning and scheduling at a shipyard that built and repaired vessels for the navy. My responsibilities included the chairing of daily planning meetings with the yard's test engineer, the engineering officer, regulatory representatives from the navy, trade supervisors, prime contractor representatives, quality assurance, and, on rare occasions, the ship's captain and a vice president of the shipyard. In total, there might be up to thirty individuals at the meeting, which would last usually no more than twenty minutes. During the course of the meeting, current propulsion plant status was discussed, as were the work plans for the next two days. Any new discrepancies (a nice word for problems) were delegated for resolution, and I was responsible for maintaining and publishing an updated status on all discrepancies. With all of this material to cover, the meetings still lasted only about twenty minutes. I was not a natural for running tight meetings, but the organization would tolerate nothing else—I learned quickly and also became a believer.

This responsibility forced me to work closely with all responsible individuals, and it forced me quickly to gain a comprehensive understanding of the project. Since that time, I continue to be amazed at how poorly other organizations often run their meetings and how they fail to use planning meetings as a mechanism for acquainting new hires with the business.

In order to understand a business well, you must see it from several informed perspectives. The perspectives of sales, procurement, design, money flow, and the customer have been considered here. This is important for the new employee, but it is not sufficient to provide employees with a broad perspective. To continue their development program, it is essential for them to see upper management working on important business issues. It is also necessary that they have completed the groundwork of the previous steps prior to meeting with business leadership and that they show full respect for the manager's schedule.

Anthony Jay of Video Arts Ltd., a London-based producer of training films, wrote an excellent paper (1976) about managing meetings.

Step 12: The Flow of Money   All employees ought to understand what the balance sheet and the income statement are, and yet very few do. Specifically, they need to understand these reports as they relate to your business unit, and someone needs to explain what each entry means, how business decisions are made for the purpose of improving these statements, and how the entries and decisions can impact net earnings and profit.

To stress an important point, give employees one dollar in pennies to be treated as income. If 70 percent of your business is commercial and 30 percent is defense-related, have them obtain seventy cents from the commercial sales unit and the rest from defense.

Next, have them distribute those portions, penny by penny, to cover expenses, wages, and capital spending—requiring them to discuss these expenditures with the appropriate personnel. Have them deduct taxes; finally, let them keep the profit that is left over—once all financial commitments are met.

Step 13: A Reading Program   I have frequently cited the need for employees to seek a larger understanding of the business; it is only with increased understanding that the opportunities come alive for them. Companies can be fairly closed environments in their philosophy and in their awareness of external matters. Any reading that will further expose your employees to technological development, economic conditions, market developments, new management practices, and the performance of specific industries may allow them to offer greater planning support and better run interference for you on developing problems.

Employees should be held accountable for reading and understanding company publications, including promotional literature, annual and quarterly reports, and, depending on your business, operations or maintenance manuals. Provide them with relevant articles published in trade and business journals and share with them as much information as you can regarding your correspondence.

> *The man who does not read good books has no*
> *advantage over the man who can't read them.*
>   Mark Twain

The most influential leader for whom I have worked required all his managers to keep reading files for all incoming and outgoing correspondence. In our business of servicing nuclear power plants, everyone traveled extensively, and it was fairly easy to catch up on business when my boss and peers all had reading files available for review. Two hours in the office on a Saturday morning made up for a long time on the road.

Step 14: Report and Presentation   It is critical that the preceding steps achieve their full impact, and this can be accomplished only by making the necessary parties accountable for satisfactory completion of each step. By requiring employees to assimilate, compile, and analyze an extensive amount of relevant business information and by also requiring them to deliver their findings to upper management by formal presentation and in a written report, a positive stress is imposed upon them and their respective supervisors to see the task through to satisfactory completion. The supervisor plays a critical role in helping the employee assemble the report and prepare the presentation. Accordingly, supervisory personnel share accountability with the individual completing a successful delivery.

> *Those having torches will pass them on to others.*
> Plato

The presentation and report should be reviewed by a blue ribbon panel of top level managers. Here is where they will assess the development of each participating employee and supervisor. Only they can set the performance standards high enough to make sure that successful completion is broadly recognized as an important accomplishment.

Feedback from Recent Hires

Recent alumni were eager to respond to our questionnaire regarding their career experiences. Overall, their responses reflected careful deliberation. It is clear that starting a career demanded their full attention, and I was impressed with the extent they seemed to understand effectively their relationships with the organization and their will to provide detailed information that would contribute proactively.

They identified several aspects of their work to be most satisfying. Indeed, the content of their responses was weighted much more heavily to what they liked rather than what they disliked:

Most satisfying to them was gaining new knowledge, skills, and training. It was for them, perhaps, the most clear indicator of their development and growing utility to the organization.

A sense of importance, contribution, and/or responsibility was almost as important. In their minds, this offered them the first tangible feeling that they were earning their pay and meeting a need within the organization.

Helping others and benefiting customers was essential. Although similar to the preceding comment, I see this as an example of employees not only meeting a need, but also establishing their own value or need within the organization.

Teamwork allowed them to establish contacts and utilize the experience of others to assist in their development. It was implied that work of a project nature was enjoyed and that few really wanted to be loners.

In seeming contrast to the preceding, individuals were equally expressive in desiring independence on the job. I do not believe this is in conflict, however. Individuals want the independence to accomplish their work with some creativity and see that the product of their efforts is not only useful to the organization, but also is uniquely their contribution.

Challenge was important. Engineering graduates are conditioned to meet challenge as a means toward testing themselves and establishing their abilities for additional responsibility or recognition. They wish to establish themselves competitively within in a competitive environment. Although team participation is a goal, employees also desire eventually to become first among equals when considering their peers.

Technical problem solving and decision making were important. After four or more years of engineering education, the graduates see this as the ultimate opportunity to validate themselves as engineers—actually to design or build something that someone else will use. It is a natural extension of their educational interests and conditioning.

Financial reward appeared somewhat later in their responses. Although views naturally range considerably among individual responses, rate of pay was generally less important to recent hires than the items just listed.

Among the adverse elements of a job were corporate politics, negative people, hours, poor economic conditions, low sense of self-worth, limited or nonexistent promotional opportunities, and, further down the list, pay. It seemed that items raised were specific to the individual and his or her employer, so it is difficult to draw broad conclusions. I would venture that concerns raised are also highly dependent upon where the individual employee is in his or her own development and maturity.

New hires considered job-related flexibility to be important, and most felt they had moderate flexibility at work. I find that recent hires can fail to see the opportunities for growth, variety, and change that exist for them at work. It is worthwhile to discuss their perspectives on flexibility and perhaps draw examples from other employees who successfully incorporated flexibility into their job responsibilities.

What do they want from you as a good manager?

Above all else, they want you to listen well. Listening well does not necessarily mean listening a lot, but it does mean seeking to understand. Good listening skills have elements of both substance and image. It is easy for busy mangers to close the topic of conversation once they believe they understand what point is being made. Not much more effort or time is needed to convince others that their comments matter to you and that you want to understand their points completely.

Good communications was a strong second factor. Communication clearly overlaps with the first trait of a good manager, in their eyes. The desired qualities of a good manager are listed in Figure 5.2.

The characteristics identified by recent graduates for a good organization are excellent. I believe responses shown in Figure 5.3 reflect maturity and goodwill for the organization on the part of the respondents. These attributes are evident in the value placed on financial stability of the organization, commitment to the customer and to quality, management foresight to avoid problems and capitalize upon business opportunities, market position, and corporate attitude.

It is apparent that synergistic opportunity exists, where your concerns and needs complement those of your employees. They really want for the organization the same things you do, and you also share similar desires for their growth and increased contribution.

With your authority, you have the chance to design a better program for their development that will also better suit the needs of your organization. However, you will have to commit organizational resources to the task, and you must hold the process and its team members accountable for the performance that the program can realize.

As employees meet with your key people, they should prepare an agenda of questions and share it with the person with

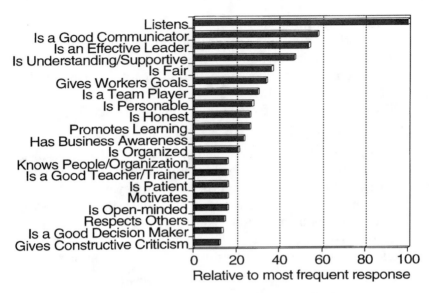

Fig. 5.2 Characteristics of a Good Manager

whom they are scheduled to meet. When each meeting or interview is scheduled, it should be limited to no more than twenty minutes, and the new hires must always recognize the need for scheduling to be at the convenience of the manager. When meetings are conducted, the employees should see that meetings do not exceed the allotted time, unless specifically requested by the other individual (manager). After the meeting, employees should prepare a set of notes documenting the meeting discussion and follow up with a note of thanks if they met with customers or individuals from other divisions.

Within your business unit, employees should meet with leadership personnel that have responsibilities for engineering, manufacturing, sales and marketing, finance, quality, and human resources. These meetings are a challenge for management. First, some employees will only regurgitate the party line and are reluctant to share their own observations. This reluctance can result from any of several factors but often reflects insecurity on the managers' part. They may not want someone looking over their shoulders, or they may doubt their own leadership abilities.

To help keep the interview fruitful, they should consider the following kinds of questions:

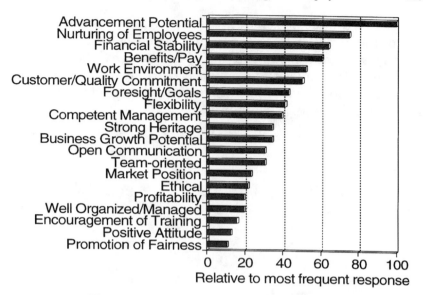

Fig. 5.3 Characteristics of a Good Company

1. What do you find most interesting about your responsibilities and this industry?

2. In meeting your current responsibilities, what experiences and education have played a critical role for you?

3. A lot of people do not get to your level; why do you think you did rather than someone else?

4. Describe the qualities of an ideal employee in your organization. How do you see that individual progressing under you as a new hire?

5. Regarding the business, what are your principal concerns regarding the future?

6. Do you have recommended dos and don'ts for new employees? If so, what are they?

7. What do you see as the most important opportunities for business growth? Conversely, what are the biggest risks we face in the next five years?

8. Are there other people in the organization with whom you recommend I talk? Who are they, and what do they do?

As you can see, the effort is to get away from a sterile discussion of the company mission statement and place emphasis on the leadership as a group of living, thinking individuals. The effort is more than a visit; the employee/participant is going to be held accountable for an increased understanding of the market, the business, and its leadership.

Chapter 6

Making Teams Work

> Treat people as if they were what
> they ought to be and you help
> them to become what they are
> capable of being.

Johann W. von Goethe

One might hope that work would always be enjoyable and fulfilling, that good decision making would be democratic in nature (or at least eventually popular), and that employees would like everything about what they do and with whom they work. Such a hope is not only unrealistic, but also misguided. The work atmosphere should be constructive rather than comfortable for each member. The processes and decisions of leadership must be respected, regardless of their popularity. In this realm, stress can serve a critical role in the development of people and business. Tension forces the individual toward deliberate thought; individual development (i.e., growth in understanding, ability, and even attitude) must be preceded by deliberate thought; and the paramount ability for an organization to prosper is contingent upon the quality (development) of its members as individuals. Stress is a motivation for change and must be channeled for change to be constructive. Organizations place stress on the individual to meet organizational goals; with adequate forethought, this stress ought to encourage individual development as well.

Consider Susan, who was appointed manager of the power systems robotics group just over a year ago. Among her group of sixty-two are seven supervisors who report to her and who hold responsibilities for electrical, mechanical, and software design, integrated testing, procedures (operation, testing, troubleshooting, and maintenance), and field support. In turn, Susan reports to her director, Aaron Bloom, along with several other managers. Susan's group serves the nuclear power industry and is the largest of three robotic business units. Another group is dedicated to defense-related work for the government, and the third has offshore contracts, most of which relate to oil exploration. The other four managers support the robotic systems efforts with end-effector, controls, and business development.

Susan's year, so far, has been both good and bad. With a year's experience under her belt, she finds the challenges of this new position stimulating, but she sees that her group's progress is not what she had expected it would be. Business remains slow, and a shake-out continues in the industry. Hence the possibilities of cutbacks and consolidation are clearly in the cards. These conditions would, of themselves, serve to stifle progress and enthusiasm, but it is apparent to her that she also has not been effective in planning and implementing improvements. She had wanted to establish herself quickly as a leader with a track record of success and expected that results would be evident within a year's time. This goal has not been met to her satisfaction. She is used to exceeding expectations and finds current circumstances uncomfortable. Susan has a strong sense of being observed from all directions. Her management promoted her to this position with a hope for change and improvement in her group and because they believed that she offered the most opportunity as a change agent.

The bright side isn't fully evident to Susan at the moment, but there are aspects of being manager she enjoys:

1. For the first time, Susan has authority to direct the efforts of a group. As a supervisor, her primary role was the delegation and monitoring of work among individuals; she had little control over what or how work was accomplished. In the role of supervisor, Susan felt fully reactive in carrying out her responsibilities. As manager, she now sees room for proactive measures, but she is challenged to develop her group's ability to think strategically. As engineer, she worked on the tasks given her. As supervisor, she delegated most of the work to others and saw the work to its satisfactory completion. Now she spends at least some time trying to plan strategically.

2. Susan enjoys an increased availability of strategic information. Although the extent of this information is still quite limited, it is sensitizing her more to the business pressures on management, and she is gaining important insight regarding business operation and the strengths and weaknesses of decision making at the top. She

sees that the difficulties in communicating information among the various management and working levels are greater than she would have expected.

3. Susan is formulating an understanding of the talents and interests existing within her group. The concept of motivating others still seems alien to her. After all, don't people become engineers because they are already self-motivated? As a supervisor, it had seemed that the group could make headway in its operational efficiency. Yet progress under her leadership remains evasive. Although the goals have not been realized, Susan is getting an education. Motivation is one subject she has yet to master.

4. She is gaining a sense of independence relative to her peer managers. Although peer acceptance seems critical when you first accept the responsibilities of a new position, the emphasis of her deliberations continues to shift toward the performance and well-being of her group, and that is really what her peers want of her as well.

Partly because the environment contains a blend of stress, change, and uncertainty and partly because her leadership shows no evident gain yet, Susan chooses to play her hand carefully. The dark side of her year is that she can offer little tangible progress and no clear plan for the future.

Whether reticent or undecided, her reluctance to communicate is propagating downward in her group. The large number of variables is overwhelming to Susan, and she is having difficulty formulating a plan for identifying and implementing improvements. Her time for trial and error is coming to a close, and she must soon demonstrate her mettle.

The company had experienced several years of mild contraction, which resulted in budget cuts and attrition. These initial reductions resulted primarily from early retirements and resignations, rather than layoffs. These decreases were appropriate and had little impact on the structure and function of the organization. Thus, they were reasonably well accepted by the remaining employees. Persisting market weakness suggests that more fundamental changes, such as reorganization and consolidation of business efforts, are next. This is the rumor being passed around, and layoffs are anticipated in engineering.

Bjorn Thompson, vice president of operations, attended Aaron's Monday morning staff meeting to announce a need for restructuring:

Our overall business is down about 17 percent from two years ago, and engineering and design activity is down by almost 20 percent. Part of this we believe is cyclic, and part of it reflects a fundamental shift in the market. The new project with RRVT has finally been signed, but with a more relaxed schedule and a somewhat reduced scope of work. Work on this project will not start for another six months. Our other projects efforts are continuing as expected, and follow-on work seems to be increasing slightly.

It is apparent that we must trim operating costs, but it is also imperative for the organization to function more efficiently and with greater flexibility. I believe that this can be realized only through a rethinking of organizational structure and practices. It may seem natural that further staff reductions will follow, but these actions ought necessarily to follow the development of strategy. Cutbacks and restructuring tend to be highly reactive in nature. That bothers me. We may be forced to "right-size," but we, as management, are paid to strengthen a business, not shrink it.

I am requesting that each of you review your group's operation and explore opportunities for consolidating efforts, improving coordination with other groups, and implementing a more aggressive program for employee development. I should not pick on any one area, but as an example, we have two junior engineers in nuclear robotics who have not yet established themselves as members of our team. I decided to read their performance reviews to see what problems might exist and found that their reviews are several months overdue. In other groups, completed personnel reviews often contain little information of proactive value. Other problems of similar scope also exist, but I remain convinced that each group faces important openings for improvement. My area also holds responsibility. I should have been more directly involved in your development as mangers, and I should have certainly kept abreast of all performance reviews. The good news is that the economic climate has finally forced change. We must correct old problems and adopt more effective practices. We have no choice but to improve upon our current operational practices.

Do not misunderstand me; the number of managers and operating groups will likely be reduced, the organization needs a plan, and I need to find out which of you has the acumen for understanding strategic growth possibilities in the context of current business constraints. I want each of you to prepare an assessment of current business conditions, followed by a strategic plan for our business. This is the initial step toward reforming our operation, and it also help me identify those managers who will best be able to assume the leadership responsibilities that will see us into the future. Each of you has important abilities in regard to our business needs. I have no plans to put any of you on the street. Those of you who are not selected for managerial slots will be otherwise utilized. In the face of the current uncertainty, your support is critical to the success of the effort. I need your best thinking, and I need you to get your respective groups behind this planning effort.

JUST A LITTLE REORGANIZATION, KIND OF A MID-COURSE CORRECTION...ONCE WE FIGURE OUT OUR NEW MISSION AND GOALS, WE'LL BE RIGHT ON TRACK.

> I should also announce here that Sampson Davis has decided to
> pursue a career change and attend seminary. His contributions here
> are lasting and his help will be missed. Sampson is one of the finest
> engineers and managers I have worked with and I certainly wish him
> every success in all his pursuits.

Susan was taken by surprise. She and her group had been singled out for
failing to bring new hires on line. It seems obvious that her management
instead ought to be helping her get on her feet, and it seems just as evident
that her supervisors should have stepped forward to assume their responsibilities for getting the new hires on line. Here she is, holding the bag, and if
she doesn't set a direction and make some visible progress fairly soon, her
group may become history.

She was tense and angry when she left the meeting and chose not to
discuss the challenge with any of her staff until she could put the matter in
perspective. That night she called her father to talk over the day's events. He
might be the one to help her find a solution.

If she was looking for sympathy, she found little. "I'd like to be able to
talk with you about this as your father, but I feel that fatherly compassion will
do you more harm than good. Your organization is looking for help, and you
must reach beyond your current limitations if you are to become part of the
solution instead of part of the problem. This should prove to be a time of
growth for you—if being a manager was supposed to be easy, then anyone
could be one. You had best make yourself needed, and thus you must also
understand what is wanted and what is needed."

Susan commented that she didn't understand and her father responded,
"You're right. You don't understand. Look at the individuals you mentioned
having difficulty with. Have you thought about what they need? They are
probably as consumed with organizational stress as you are. What do they
need, and how can you help them?" A little annoyed with her father's response, Susan then inquired as to how she might learn these things. "You
cannot, by yourself, reason out what others worry about and what they want.
They must tell you, and it is your responsibility to make them want to share
with you their perspectives—you have not done that." She wondered to
herself why she also wasn't thinking about attending seminary.

A wry twist! Susan's engineering career seemed the model of success,
yet none of her current problems were engineering problems. Not one of her
college courses related to the issues of individuals, groups, and business strategy she was facing. These were now the issues that would now make or
break her career, and no one told her how or when to prepare for them!
Could she become at once the epitome of an engineering success and management failure? On top of it all, her father was talking in parables. After the

phone call, she pondered her challenge a little further but still with more questions than answers.

The next morning Susan arrived at the office with a resolve to understand and address the challenges she faced. Enough was riding on her performance that she had little to lose in pursuing some difficult issues with those with whom she worked. She was prepared to be candid with them regarding her concerns, and she was determined to make sense out of the current situation. Susan's agenda included several items. First, she met with her supervisors to discuss the previous day's meeting, the need to complete the reviews effectively, and the need to start looking for positive steps to be taken. Susan took responsibility for the lack of addressing individual needs or organizational planning. She made it clear that she was expecting much more of her supervisors as a result of yesterday's meeting—not because the vice president demanded it, but because he made Susan recognize what she should have been doing all along with her group.

A few days later she started a series of meetings with her group to acquaint them with the facts of the current climate and to help quash unproductive rumors. She intended to involve various engineers with the upcoming efforts to improve effectiveness and productivity of the organization. Susan also reached out to Aaron with her questions and her concerns. She was much more open in presenting her views and her questions, and she found Aaron to be a valuable resource of information and perspective.

There were other steps taken as Susan pursued every lead that might help her better prepare herself and her group for the changes ahead. It was apparent that her efforts were in search of solutions and opportunities.

Was she successful? It matters only that she eventually assumed her responsibilities and exercised her control in leading people and managing an operation. The wake-up call came from her vice president, and she, in turn, put herself and her group into action.

Did she need the jolt from her management? To the extent that she had not previously taken a proactive role, she clearly did. However, it would have been preferable for all had she recognized the need for action sooner and on her own. Regardless what subsequently happens in Susan's career, she will not likely repeat her mistakes of this year.

Was her management at fault? I believe they erred in several ways: They allowed problems to develop; perhaps a planning effort should already have been in progress; and they had not emphasized the importance of reviews or of management development. Possibly their actions resulted from pressure applied by their management or by the board of directors. From Susan's perspective, it would be counterproductive to dwell on errors her management may have made. The one person's actions over which she has most control are her own, and she had ample opportunity to increase her managerial effectiveness.

How relevant is it that Susan was recently promoted to manager? It is relevant that she was new and inexperienced in her responsibilities; it is not really relevant that she is a manager. After all, the nature of her problems is quite similar to the root of José's problems—lack of communications, knowledge and awareness.

Can an individual wake up an organization? You are responsible for helping the organization as much as you can, but it is not your responsibility to tell your management how to manage. I would expect you to be much more successful in modifying your own actions and the actions of those under your supervision. It is difficult for you to accomplish this kind of change with management and with peers. People who are effective at this demonstrate considerable understanding of both people and business—polish and sales ability.

Regarding the individual and the corporate, one does not naturally meet the needs of another just because it is a good thing to do. Needs exist with each individual and at each level of the organization. The incentives generated by the organization exist in the form of stress and are, we hope, positive in nature. This stress provides the proactive fiber that weaves individual needs into a productive system. Properly woven, one person or one level need not gain at the expense of another. The role of leadership is to find and promote synergistic avenues of collaboration among individuals and the corporate leaders.

Consider a mid-level individual with supervisory responsibilities that is seeking to further her career growth. Relative to her management, she should benefit if she can offer abilities and accomplishments that are uniquely hers—her value to the organization increases. Accordingly, it is natural for her to self-develop unique valuable qualifications that set her apart from others.

Further, she will also be well-served if she promotes the development of all subordinates in a manner that offers her the best performance and flexibility. One way to accomplish this is by promoting interchangeability among subordinates. Cross-compatibility is achieved by selecting the best characteristics among a group of individuals as a benchmark for others. In a situation where each employee is striving to expand his or her own unique value and where supervision also seeks to elevate each subordinate in ways that promote interchange, we find an organization in growth. Group ability increases, individuals grow, and flexibility is promoted.

Growth is necessarily stress-driven, but not everyone perceives these stresses as positive influences. You as an individual must determine to understand your work environment in a way that accommodates your career desires, which means meeting the needs of others. Each promotion will challenge you to understand, function, and contribute at new levels of responsibility, stress, and opportunity. Your success in any role is no one's responsibility but your own—that is the good news.

Appendix A

Career Reflections: A Survey of Recent Graduates

Dudley and Wells (1992)

Introduction

In a recent survey, individuals in the first five years of their careers (graduating classes of 1986 through 1991) reflect upon their developing views regarding bosses, companies, and definitions of success. Almost all responses were offered within the context of change from college to career. All respondents are graduates of Clarkson University's Interdisciplinary Engineering and Management Program.

Notable among the results are the coincident establishment of clear career goals with the accrual of experience, the evolving definition of success from fame and fortune to competence and contribution, and the general sense of mission that seemed to permeate the 245 responses. The questionnaire comprised two kinds of questions. One set of questions sought feedback that could easily be quantified (multiple choice, ranking, and short answer), and a corresponding set allowed the respondent to express, in a more open format, opinions and observations regarding career-related issues. Both sets of questions yielded considerable information for analysis.

This paper summarizes the results of this survey and highlights that information that may be of interest to either of two groups: those who are in the early years of their career or those industrial leaders who are responsible for hiring and developing new talent.

Objective

Many resources in the form of counseling and written material exist to help individuals select and pursue educational goals. Further, many other resources are available to help the individual pursue development as a professional or as a corporate leader. However, beyond the policies and practices of an employer, few resources exist to help the individual with his or her initial years on the job. This survey sought information that would help college seniors gain a more complete and effective understanding of the workplace in industry. This information may be particularly relevant for graduates in the current competitive business environment. The purpose of this study was to collect information to meet the following objectives:

1. Help college seniors develop a more realistic perspective of what awaits them in their careers.
2. Determine the views of recent graduates on topics ranging from relocation to graduate study.
3. Seek recent graduate's perspectives on desirable positions, managers, and employers.

Survey Questionnaire and Response

The questionnaire was four pages in length and contained twenty-nine questions, some with multiple parts. It was decided that the questionnaire should have both qualitative and quantitative components, and it was estimated that the questionnaire would require about twenty-five minutes to complete.

The majority of respondents gave in-depth and often lengthy answers to the questions requesting written comments. Few individuals left any questions blank, and it was evident that career development was a topic of high importance to the respondent. Questions inviting written answers often drew numerous specific points. By categorizing and tabulating the components of these written responses, specific points were identified and prioritized.

Results

Setting and Meeting Goals

Only one-third of the respondents had specific career goals during their senior year job search. As may be expected, work experience had a penetrating influence, with three-quarters of the respondents now having definite career goals. Only two respondents had migrated from having goals at graduation to having none currently. The following comments are representative of the responses received:

Realize through work what one likes or dislikes.

Have become more focused, yet more realistic.

Experience has lead to goals.

Job has changed goals—clearer views.

Been following goals; knew what I wanted and went after it.

How does one better define their career goals? The most common recommendations included the following:

Get experience to determine your goals.

Research companies and get counseling.

Make contacts in your area of interest.

Be open-minded.

Determine what you want and go after it.

Learn as much as possible.

Make sure you're happy.

Talk to alumni.

It is reassuring to note that 94 percent indicated that they were making progress toward career goals. Curiously, this response exceeds the 75 percent who currently have clear goals.

What to Look for in a Job

When asked to comment on the nature of a good organization or a good boss, voluntary responses were quite detailed. In descending order are listed the most desirable traits to look for in an employer and a supervisor/manager. The frequency with which particular comments were offered are listed in parentheses:

The Good Boss

Listens (76)
Communicates (44)
Shows leadership (41)
Understands and is supportive (36)
Is fair (28)
Gives workers goals (26)
Is a team player (23)
Is personable (21)
Guides/lets you learn (20)
Is honest (20)
Has job knowledge (18)
Is organized (16)
Is open-minded (12)
Is patient (12)
Is a good teacher/trainer (12)
Knows what is going on (12)
Motivates (12)
Respects others (11)
Is an effective decision-maker (10)
Provides constructive criticism (9)

The Good Organization

Has advancement opportunities (56)
Shows care for employees (42)
Is financially stable (36)
Has good pay/benefits (34)
Creates a pleasant work environment (29)
Is commited to customers and quality (28)
Has foresight/corporate goals (24)
Offers flexibility (23)
Has competent or good management (22)
Has a solid history/heritage (19)
Realizes growth and expansion (19)
Is team-oriented (17)
Promotes open communications (17)
Has good market position (13)
Has ethical integrity (12)
Is well-organized/managed (11)
Is profitable (11)
Provides good training (9)
Promotes a positive attitude (7)
Values fairness (6)

Getting the Job, Getting the Promotion

Recent graduates indicate that motivation is the most important trait their employer seeks when recruiting talent. A willingness to learn, communication skills, confidence, punctuality, independence, and being well-rounded are also considered critical. When measuring job performance, recent graduates note that productivity and responsibility are emphasized most by employers. Additional areas of importance include judgment, teamwork, profitability, leadership, and accuracy of work.

To Do or Not to Do

What can get in the way of a successful career or job start? What should be done once clear goals are established? The dos and don'ts are listed here.

What Works

Commit to goals

Be open-minded and confident

Work hard, do your best

Utilize contacts, network

Go after dreams

Enjoy life and have fun

Don't limit yourself

Don't fear change

Be selective

Take risks and be flexible

Be candid/honest

What Doesn't Work

Bad attitude

Poor motivation/not aggressive

Poor economic conditions

Close-mindedness

The wrong job

Personal limitations/ inflexibility

Inability—poor experience/ skills/training

Lack of mentor/no direction

Uncaring boss

Not having goals

Tardiness/missed deadlines

Flexibility at Work

Nine out of ten respondents placed importance on job and/ or career flexibility. Fortunately, the average respondent felt a moderate to strong degree of flexibility in his or her current position. When asked to describe the nature of flexibility, the following comments were representative:

Qualified for multiple / changing job roles.

Broad responsibilities and experience.

Control over career path.

Adaptability to new situations and people.

Willingness to develop and try other functions.

Career Satisfaction

Most survey responses included extensive feedback regarding career satisfaction. The results of the most and least satisfying aspects of a job are listed here (with the most frequent responses at the top):

Most Satisfying Aspects	Least Satisfying Aspects
Knowledge gained	Corporate politics
Sense of contribution/ responsibility	Negative co-workers
Helping customers/benefiting others	Hours on the job
Teamwork	Economy/layoffs
Job independence	Low sense of worth
Challenge	Stress/pressure
Problem solving/decision making	Limited growth opportunity
Constant change/diversity	Paperwork/tedium
Meeting objectives	Financial reward
Financial reward	Routine

The definition of success seems to evolve significantly from college to the career environment. Although it seems easy to revert to money and position as accepted aspects of success, once the professional career commences, a change in perspective seems to tie success more closely with the environment and success of the organization. The most frequently cited components of career success (descending order) included these:

Personal happiness
Responsibility and
   contribution
Right balance in life
Upward mobility
Learning
Realizing personal growth

Job satisfaction
Financial reward
Challenge
Meeting personal goals
Meeting career goals

Job-Related Stress

Respondents were asked if they considered their responsibilities to be stressful. Also, their views were sought regarding whether stress has a positive or a negative role in their careers. Respondents reported that their responsibilities were quite stressful, but they were divided in their opinions of stress as a positive influence in their personal careers. In aggregate, stress was identified as a slightly positive factor in their personal and professional development.

Changing Jobs and Relocation

The average respondent had graduated 3 ½ years earlier and had changed companies one time. Currently, 17 percent of the respondents are actively seeking to change employers.

Survey results were evenly divided as to the personal importance of location in pursuing a career opportunity. Of the 186 respondents who did relocate from their college and home towns, 96 percent indicated that the experience of relocation was a strongly positive one, even though some noted that relocation is not easy.

Graduate Studies

The pursuit of graduate studies was considered moderately important (scale choices included none, slight, moderate, and strong), but 87 percent indicated that work experience should precede the pursuit of graduate studies.

Seventy-three percent of all respondents intend to complete graduate work. Twelve percent have already completed a graduate program, and an additional 27 percent have graduate work currently in progress. Primary fields of interest include MBA, engineering (various disciplines), law, medicine, and education. Twenty percent of all respondents do not plan to pursue graduate work.

Retrospective: Free Electives

Recent graduates pursuing a career in industry appear quite pragmatic in their views on education. Regarding the selection of free electives, the five predominant areas recommended as important indicate communications (oral and written), followed by engineering, management, and marketing. It is likely that such recommendations are quite dependent upon major, current functional responsibilities, and where the individual is in his or her career path. Individuals in the later phases of their careers could, for example, indicate a greater emphasis on the arts and humanities. This issue is beyond the scope of this study.

A Common Denominator

During the analysis of data, an effort was made to uncover significant correlations among the responses to various topical areas. Clearly, there was only one issue that related strongly to many other subjects. That single issue was the individual's perception of stress as a positive or negative influence in his or her career.

Individuals who perceive stress as a positive or constructive element in their work were much more likely to have done the following:

Established career goals.

Make progress toward goals.

Value a sense of contribution at work.

Have a sense of flexibility in their work.

Have entrepreneurial plans and/or accomplishments.

Conclusion

1. Recent graduates give their careers considerable thought and willingly share their views and experiences. This is

evident in the high response rate and the quality of written detail offered in response to many of the questions.

2. Because of the role of experience, most individuals tend to develop career goals after graduation. A significant majority expressed a sense of developmental progress in their personal/career growth.

3. Perspectives change regarding success. Students often lack a clear or tangible definition of career success and satisfaction. A working definition evolves in the workplace that often comes to include contribution, competence, and flexibility as important components.

4. A vast majority of those who relocated (by choice or otherwise) viewed the experience as a strongly positive one.

5. Those who viewed job-related stress as a positive influence for them were more likely to have goals, be entrepreneurial, be making progress toward goals, and place importance on their abilities to make contributions.

Appendix B

Reading Worth Considering

A few resources are listed here for your reference. Some of these materials I have happened upon by myself, and others were recommended by people who understood my interest in the topic of career management and were aware of my efforts to write on the subject. I am deeply grateful for their continuuing vigilance in seeking to keep me informed and honest.

I have looked at all the materials and offer my own observations. If my comments are brief, then you may conclude that the resource, may be worthwhile but perhaps not directly related to this book. I hope that you will find this information of use; I would greatly appreciate your recommendations for other materials that have been overlooked or that have yet to be published.

Adams, James L. *Flying Butresses, Entropy, and O-Rings*. Cambridge, Mass.: Harvard University Press, 1991.

> Content: Offers a broad view on the discipline and practice of engineering. Topics include historical perspective and an overview of the engineering process from invention and de-

sign through testing, failure analysis, manufacture, markets and regulation.

Comment: The book offers an interesting view on the profession of engineering in the United States, and numerous examples are provided to illustrate and support many of the various points made. However, the book offers only limited assistance for the individual seeking career-related advice.

Asher, Donald. *From College to Career: Entry Level Résumés for any Major*. Berkeley: Ten Speed Press, 1992.

Content: Résumés, both good and bad, are explained within the larger context of the job search. The bulk of the book includes examples with excellent discussion.

Comment: Excellent. A number of résumés offer a wide variety of approaches to the search effort. Of all the books available on résumé writing, this is one of the few that has my respect. His book is an education.

Asher, Donald. *The Overnight Job Change Strategy*. Berkeley: Ten Speed Press, 1993.

Content: Identifying and developing job leads, interviewing, closing the deal, and job-search troubleshooting are some of the topics included.

Comment: The book starts on the right track with Chapter 1, "A Job Search is a Sales and Marketing Project." I believe Asher is one of the most knowledgeable and capable authors, in this area, and I find his books are on target and to the point. His recommendations may overlap with a number of others, but he offers among the most directly helpful resources on changing positions once an individual knows what he or she wants.

Asher, Donald. *The Overnight Résumé*. Berkeley: Ten Speed Press, 1992.

Content: The role of the résumé, résumé writing, getting

interviews, and cover letters are included, but the focus is, naturally, on résumé writing.

Comment: Excellent, one of the better resources for writing résumés.

Augustine, N. R. *Managing Projects and Programs*. Boston: Harvard Business School Press, 1989.

Content: Evaluating, organizing, leading, planning and controlling

Comment: Good resource on the topics of project management, terminating projects, project teams, financing, false economies, and project appraisals.

Babcock, Daniel L. *Managing Engineering and Technology*. Englewood Cliffs, NJ: Prentice Hall, 1991.

Content: In text book format, the major sections include "Introduction to Engineering Management," "Functions of Technology Management," "Product Life Cycle," "Project Management," and "Career Management."

Comment: Contains much good information in a very readable format. Developed as a resource for teaching engineering management.

Badawy, M. K. *Developing Managerial Skills in Engineers and Scientists*. New York: Van Nostrand Reinhold, 1982.

Content: The book has major parts on the transformation of engineers into managers, succeeding as a manager, and the functions of supervision, organizing, planning, and control.

Comment: I like this book. It is quite challenging, and I agree with many of the points made by the author. It has a nice section on the troublesome transition to management, and "Why the MBA Is the Wrong Degree for You" is one example of challenge. Needless to say, I don't ascribe to all of the views offered, but the author has my respect for hitting topics directly.

Beer, David F. (editor). *Writing and Speaking in the Technology*

Professions: A Practical Guide. Piscataway, NJ: IEEE Press, 1991.

> Content: A collection of reprinted IEEE papers covering the topics of writing first drafts, graphics, organization, manuals, proposals, editing, oral presentations, and managing meetings.
>
> Comment: This worthwhile collectin offers several perspectives on most of the important topics. It is a credible source of information and advice and, as a resource on business communications, will be an asset to individuals and organizations alike.

Blanchard, K. and S. Johnson. *The One Minute Manager.* New York: William Morrow, 1982.

> Content: Story of interaction between an excellent manager and an individual who wants to learn more about this remarkable individual.
>
> Comment: An outstanding perpective on management presented simply in story. It is a short book that can be devoured in an evening but deserves much greater consideration.

Bolles, Richard Nelson, *The 1994 What Color is Your Parachute?* Berkeley: Ten Speed Press, 1994.

> Content: Broad headings include "Putting Things in Perspective," "Job Hunting," "Choosing or Changing a Career," "Securing and Conducting an Interview Successfully," a highly useful collection of appendices, and a wonderful epilogue titled "How to Find Your Mission in Life."
>
> Comment: This is the preeminent book on the topic of career change for good reason—the information provided is comprehensive and highly useful for the individual. It is updated annually and provides the reader a wealth of information on setting and pursuing career-related goals. As a resource, it is as valuable to the recent graduate as it is for mid-career individuals considering change.

Cole, Kenneth J. *The Headhunter Strategy.* New York: John Wiley, 1985.

Content: Topical headings include "Groundwork," "Job Search," and "Headhunter Strategy," with a focus on working with headhunters and their perspectives on job hunting.

Comment: This book came highly recommended, and I must throw in my support for the work as well. The first chapter is titled "The Résumé Defrocked," and it is one of the few written perspectives I agree with. Cole is direct in his approach and provides important justification for the suggestions and recommendations included. He writes as one who has "lived" the process, not as one who has merely heard.

Crystal, J. C. and R. N. Bolles. *Where Do I Go From Here With My Life?* Berkeley: Ten Speed Press, 1974.

Content: "Your Autobiography," "Achievements," "Skills," "Preferences," "Aversions," "Clustering Skills," "Meeting Targets," and much more. Presented in a sequence of sixteen sessions to help the individual evaluate his or her goals and establish a plan for meeting these goals.

Comment: I was pleasantly surprised to learn that this work was funded by IEEE as a resource for the many electrical engineers facing layoffs and forced job changes during the early seventies.

Dalton, Gene W. and Paul H. Thompson. *Novations*. Glenview, Ill.: Scott, Foresman, 1986.

Content: The book identifies four relational stages of development for the professional, apprentice, colleague, mentor, and sponsor, and the book generally addresses the topics in this order.

Comment: This worthwhile book offers credible insight regarding how people perceive themselves, think about work, and relate to others. As the developing engineer assumes increased responsibility for other people, this book can be an excellent source for developing a more effective understanding of how individuals can and should interact within a functioning group. I recommend it highly for the individual seeking in earnest to become a leader.

Daoust, Tom. *Staying Employed*. Lexington, Mass.: Lexington Books, 1990.

> Content: The major sections are "The New Employment Market," "What You Must Do Before You Need to Hire an Employer," and "How to Hire a New Employer."
>
> Comment: The emphasis is naturally on finding a job and the book is comprehensive, readable, and generally helpful. I liked the short section titled "Why Personnel People Are Both Weak and Deadly."

Employment Guide for Scientists and Engineers, Vols. 1 and 2. Piscataway, NJ.: IEEE—U.S. Activities, 1991.

> Content: Volume 1 includes coping with a loss of employment, networking, writing letters and résumés, interviewing, and using employment services as well as an overview of your rights at work. Volume 2 provides a 77-page list of companies (with individual contact name, title, address, and, in some cases, phone and FAX numbers) that employ electrical engineers and might have openings.
>
> Comment: Short, to the point, a highly useful resource, and inexpensive (particularly if you belong to IEEE). The first volume contains excellent advice that is often overlooked. Volume 1 is worth reading and contemplating. The second volume provides the reader with an extensive list of potential employers, sorted geographically. As stated, the lists contain individual's names, titles, and, often, telephone numbers.

Eyler, David L. *Résumés That Mean Business*. New York: Random House, 1990.

> Content: How to write a résumé, dos and don'ts, and numerous examples comprise the bulk of this text.
>
> Comment: Thorough in its examples; it provides good advice, clearly and concisely. A good resource.

Figlar, Howard. *The Complete Job Search Handbook* (revised).

New York: Henry Holt, 1988.

> Content: The six parts of this book are "Self-Assessment Skills," "Detective Skills," "Communication Skills," "Skills for Selling Yourself," "Special Problems and Special Solutions," and "Other Perspectives."
>
> Comment: Dr. Figlar is Director of Career Placement at the University of Austin and has produced a comprehensive and highly useful work on job hunting. This book will help readers immensely in their efforts to commence a career. I hope Dr. Figlar will one day forgive me in regard to my comments about college placement/career development offices.

Germann, R., and P. Arnold. *Job and Career Building*. New York: Harper and Row, 1980; reprinted by Ten Speed Press.

> Content: This book offers a general coverage of a wide range of career-related topics, including job and career problems, objectives, various aspects of the search effort, negotiations, and career follow-through on the new job.
>
> Comment: Although the book does not specifically address career issues from an engineering or industry perspective, its broad view contains much useful information for the individual. The twelve rules for advancing one's career are excellent and are reiterated in Chapter 4.

Hitt, William D. *Management in Action*. Columbus, OH.: Battelle Press, 1985.

> Content: Topics include management philosophy, leadership, participative management, organization, staffing and staff development, and motivation.
>
> Comment: I like both of Hitt's books. In reading them, I find they cover a range of important topics, and that the insight offered is genuine and relevent. They are worthwhile resources for those seeking to understand issues related to the managemet of engineers and engineering and the motivation of individuals.

Hitt, William D. *The Leader-Manager*. Columbus, OH.: Battelle
Press, 1988.

> Content: Chapter topics include "The Nature of Leadership,"
> "The Leader as Change Agent," "Creating the Vision," "De-
> veloping the Team," "Clarifying the Values," "Positioning,"
> and others.
>
> Comment: Hitt's book offers a clear perspective on the roles
> and mechanisms of leadership. As with his other book, Hitt's
> perspectives are genuine and well worth consideration.

Jay, Antony. "How to run a meeting." *Harvard Business Review*.
Boston: (March–April 1976) 43–57 (reprint 76204).

> Content: This is a reprinted HBR paper that reviews the
> function of meetings, various types of meetings, preparations,
> and the person's responsibilities.
>
> Comment: This article is a great resource that helps to clarify
> the reason and way for conducting a meeting. Meeting man-
> agement, when properly done, is the most obvious demon-
> stration of leadership ability. As I write this now, I wonder
> why I have not previously shared this paper with those with
> and for whom I work.

Kamm, Lawrence J. *Real-World Engineering*. Piscataway, NJ.:
IEEE Press, 1991.

> Content: "Innovation and Conceptual Design," "People Prob-
> lems," "Your Knowledge Base," "Topics in Engineering De-
> sign."
>
> Comment: This text covers a wide range of topics relating to
> the profession of engineering, from patents to project man-
> agement and from finance to experimentation.

Markel, Mike. *Writing in the Technical Fields*. Piscataway, NJ.:
IEEE Press, 1994.

> Content: The book is composed of two major parts: one ad-
> dresses how to write and the other covers applications (i.e.,

letters, reports, manuals, etc.). Appendices offer helpful information on punctuation, style, common mistakes, and misused words and a checklist for commencing a writing project.

Comment: The information is useful and well presented.

Medley, H. Anthony. *Sweaty Palms: The Neglected Art of Being Interviewed*, revised edition. Berkeley: Ten Speed Press, 1992.

Content: Just about every facet of being interviewed is covered.

Comment: This book is highly rated by many and benefits the reader by maintaining a focus on the interview. I also recommend this book.

Meyer, H.E., and J. M. Meyer. *How to Write*. Washington, D.C.: Storm King Press, 1986.

Content: The principle components are preparation for writing, writing the first draft, and polishing the product.

Comment: The book is short and to the point. If you wish to have a single brief reference, *How to Write* may be the most helpful resource you, as a recent graduate, can have on writing.

Murphy, H. A., and H. W. Hildebrandt. *Effective Business Communications*, 5th ed. New York: McGraw-Hill, 1988.

Content: The material is presented in six parts: "Background for Communicating," "Major Plans for Letters and Memos," "Special Messages," "Reports," "Oral Communications," and "Significant Concerns for Effective Business Communications."

Comment: This widely used textbook provides a comprehensive introduction to business communications. Its organization makes needed material readily available, and its comprehensive coverage justifies the price.

Naisbitt, John. *Global Paradox*. New York: William Morrow, 1994.

Comment: Engineers are naturally focused individuals, and the workplace often does little to extend their view of markets, economy, and culture. *Global Paradox* introduces the reader to economic and political trends that are occurring on an international level and how they may influence companies, work and people. If you want to extend your view of the world, this book can introduce you to important issues.

Ries, A., and J. Trout. *Positioning: The Battle for Your Mind.* New York: McGraw-Hill, 1981.

Comment: The focus is on marketing and promotion, and numerous examples are used to illustrate the points made. What is interesting is that similar issues of perception relate both to the efforts of an automobile manufacturer to increase market share and to your efforts in soliciting support for ideas, plans, and designs at work.

Although some of the examples now seem a little out of date, *Positioning* offers important insight regarding the task of getting your ideas and/or products considered favorably over all others. To realize progress in this task, you must consider how your audience perceives the market and how your competition seeks to penetrate your audience. For engineers seeking to gain an understanding of the commercial side of the business, this short book offers much food for thought.

Ries, A., and J. Trout. *Marketing Warfare.* New York: McGraw-Hill, 1986.

Comment: This book provides a nice addition to the authors' first book, *Positioning*. The notion of comparing market strategy and tactics with battlefield situations is excellent. This book seems more focused, and thus obliges the reader to recognize the brutal need for understanding market pressures well enough to survive them successfully.

Vroom, V. H. et al. *Manage People, Not Personnel.* Boston: Harvard Business School Press, 1990.

Content: The broad headings of "Motivation" and "Performance Appraisal" address a range of topics, including "Human Resources," "Reward and Compensation," "Employee Growth," and "Power as a Motivator."

Comment: This collection of readings provides an effective introduction to management and organization of people.

Webber, R. A. *Becoming a Courageous Manager*. Englewood Cliffs, NJ.: Prentice-Hall, 1991.

Content: Chapter 1 is titled "Growing Up at Work," Chapter 2 is "Dealing with Early Disappointment," and Chapter 12 is "Becoming Middle-Aged in Management." There is much covered is Chapters 3 through 11 as well.

Comment: Great! Professor Webber of Wharton has produced a work that helps the readers look ahead in their careers. This book is not how to get a career started but how to make it fly. The text and case studies are unusually realistic in their approach to fundamental issues of career advancement and the assuming of increased management responsibilities in industry.

Wegman, R., R. Chapman, and M. Johnson. *Work in the New Economy*, co-published by JIST Works, Inc., and the American Association for Counseling and Development, Indianapolis, Ind., 1989.

Content: Part 1 covers economic, cultural, and employment factors that are changing how and where people work. Part 2 provides a comprehensive review of necessary job-search skills and the process of effectively penetrating an employment market. Part 3 addresses the special needs of those job-hunters who are experiencing difficulty in their search.

Comment: This book is comprehensive, well organized, and informative. Its target audience includes professionals active in career counseling or otherwise involved in issues of employment within the context of a changing economy. Accordingly, its discussion of changes currently under way in the job market is among the best I have seen.

Woelfle, Robert M. (editor). *A New Guide for Better Technical Presentations*. Piscataway, NJ.: IEEE Press, 1992.

> Content: This is a collection of papers grouped into seven parts: "Importance and Fundamentals," "Planning and Preparation," "Visual Aids," "Delivery Techniques and Tools," "Computer Graphics," "Video," and "Multimedia Presentations."
>
> Comment: The selected papers have been carefully screened, and the product is a useful reference.

References

Asher, Donald. *The Overnight Résumé*. Berkeley, CA: Ten Speed Press, 1991.

Asher, Donald. *From College to Career: Entry Level Résumés for Any Major.* Berkeley, CA: Ten Speed Press, 1992.

Asher, Donald. *The Overnight Job Change Strategy*. Berkeley, CA: Ten Speed Press, 1993.

Backe, Richard J. (editor). *Employment Guide for Engineers and Scientists.* Washington, DC: IEEE–United States Activities Office, 1991.

Bolles, Richard Nelson. *The 1994 What Color is Your Parachute?* Berkeley, CA: Ten Speed Press, 1994.

Cole, Kenneth J. *The Headhunter Strategy*. New York: John Wiley & Sons, 1985.

Daoust, Tom. *Staying Employed*. Lexington, MA: Lexington Books, 1990.

Dudley, Jody and David Wells. "Early Career Performance–Career Reflections: Classes of 1986–1991." Potsdam, NY: Clarkson University E&M Report 92-102, 1992.

Germann, R. and P. Arnold. *Job and Career Building,* New York: Harper and Row, 1980; reprinted by Ten Speed Press.

Jay, Antony. "How to run a meeting." *Harvard Business Review* (March–April 1976), Boston, MA: 43-57 (reprint 76204).

Meyer, H. E. and J. M. Meyer. *How to Write*. Washington, D.C.: Storm King Press, 1986.

Murphy, H. A. and H. W. Hildebrandt. *Effective Business Communications* 5th Edition. New York: McGraw-Hill, 1988.

Nightingale, E. *Lead the Field* (audio cassettes). Niles, IL: Nightingale-Conant Corporation, 1986.

Terkel, Studs. *Working: People Talk About What They Do All Day And How They Feel About What They Do.* New York: Pantheon Books, 1974.

Index